EMBRACING EMERGENCE
CHRISTIANITY

Phyllis Tickle
on the Church's Next Rummage Sale

A 6-SESSION STUDY BY PHYLLIS TICKLE WITH TIM SCORER

Morehouse Education Resources,
a division of Church Publishing Incorporated
Editorial Offices: 600 Grant Street, Suite 400, Denver, CO 80203

For catalogs and orders call:
1-800-242-1918
www.ChurchPublishing.org

Photos on pages 11, 26, 40, 58, 70 and 84 © Copyright 2011 by Dirk deVries. All rights reserved.
Photos on cover and page 95 © Copyright 2011 by Kelly Photography. All rights reserved.

ISBN-13: 978-1-60674-071-2

TABLE OF CONTENTS

QUICK GUIDE TO THIS HANDBOOK

TEN things to know as you begin to work with this resource:

1. HANDBOOK + WORKBOOK

This handbook is a guide to the group process as well as a workbook for everyone in the group.

2. A SIX-SESSION RESOURCE

Each of the six sessions presents a distinct topic for focused group study and conversation.

3. DVD-BASED RESOURCE

The teaching content in each session comes in the form of input by Phyllis Tickle and response by members of a small group; just over 30 minutes in length. A DVD Index is included to enable you to go directly to the section of the DVD you need.

4. EVERYONE GETS EVERYTHING

The handbook addresses everyone in the group, not one group leader. There is no separate "Leader's Guide."

5. GROUP FACILITATION

We based this resource on the understanding that someone will be designated as group facilitator for each session. You may choose the same person or a different person for each of the six sessions.

6. TIME FLEXIBILITY

Each of the six sessions is flexible and can be between one hour and two or more hours in length.

7. BUILD YOUR OWN SESSION

Each of the six sessions offers you between five and seven OPTIONS for building your own session.

8. A FORMAT WITHIN EACH OPTION

Each of the options has four consistent elements: *Opening Essay, Beginning Conversation, The Teaching,* and *Group Response to the Teaching.*

9. BEFORE THE SESSION

Each session opens with five questions for participants to consider as preparation for the session.

10. CLOSING AS IF IT MATTERS

For each session there is an option presenting a way of closing that emerges naturally from the content of the session.

BEYOND THE "QUICK GUIDE"

Helpful information and guidance for anyone using this resource:

1. HANDBOOK + WORKBOOK

This handbook is a guide to the group process as well as a workbook for everyone in the group.

- We hope the handbook gives you all the information you need to feel confident in shaping the program to work for you and your fellow group members.
- The work space provided in the handbook encourages you...
  — to respond to leading questions.
  — to write or draw your own reflections.
  — to note the helpful responses of other group members.

2. SIX-SESSION RESOURCE

This resource presents Phyllis Tickle's insights on Emergence Christianity framed as six distinct topics of study:

1. Emergence 101
2. Where Now Is Our Authority?
3. The Twentieth Century and Emergence
4. Gifts from Other Times
5. How Then Shall We Live?
6. Hallmarks of Emergence

- Although there are places of significant overlap between the six topics, we have presented each one as distinctively as possible. We hope that, by the end of the six sessions, you will have been led to fresh insights on the transformation that Christianity is undergoing in your community and country and in many other parts of the world today.

3. DVD-BASED RESOURCE

The teaching content in each session comes in the form of input by Phyllis Tickle and response by members of a small group; just over 30 minutes in length.

Phyllis Tickle's unique presentation and accessible academic authority stimulates thoughtful and heartfelt conversation among her listeners.

The edited conversations present group sharing that builds on Tickle's initial teaching. They are intended to present to you a model of small group interaction that is personal, respectful and engaged.

- You will notice that the participants in the DVD group also become our teachers. In a number of cases, quotes from the group members enrich the teaching component of this resource. This will also happen in your group; you will become teachers for one another.
- We hope that the DVD presentations spark conversations about those things that matter most to those who are walking the transformational way of Jesus in the 21st century.

4. EVERYONE GETS EVERYTHING

The handbook addresses everyone in the group, not one group leader. There is no separate "Leader's Guide."

- Unlike many small group resources, this one makes no distinction between material for the group facilitator and for the participants. Everyone has it all!
- We believe this empowers you and your fellow group members to share creatively in the leadership.

5. GROUP FACILITATION

We designed this for you to designate a group facilitator for each session. It does not have to be the same person for all six sessions, because everyone has all the material. It is, however, essential that you and the other group members are clear about who is facilitating each session. One or two people still have to be responsible for these kind of things:

- making arrangements for the meeting space (see notes on Meeting Space, p. 9)
- setting up the space to be conducive to conversations about the things that matter most
- creating and leading an opening to the session (see notes on Opening, p. 9)
- helping the group decide on which options to focus on in that session
- facilitating the group conversation for that session
- keeping track of the time
- calling the group members to attend to the standards established for the group life (see notes on Group Standards, p. 9)
- creating space in the conversation for all to participate

- keeping the conversation moving along so that the group covers all that it set out to do
- ensuring that time is taken for a satisfying closing to the session
- making sure that everyone is clear about date, location and focus for the next session
- following up with people who missed the session

6. TIME FLEXIBILITY

Each of the six sessions is flexible and can be between one hour and two or more hours in length.

- We designed this resource for your group to tailor it to fit the space available in the life of the congregation or community using it. That might be Sunday morning for an hour before or after worship, two hours on a weekday evening, or 90 minutes on a weekday morning.
- Some groups might decide to spend two sessions on one of the major topics. There's enough material in each of the six topics to do that. Rushing to get through more than the time comfortably allows, results in people not having the opportunity to speak about the things that matter most to them.

7. BUILD YOUR OWN SESSION

Each of the six sessions offers you from five to seven OPTIONS for building your own session. How will you decide what options to use?

- One or two people might take on the responsibility of shaping the session based on what they think will appeal to the group members. This responsibility could be shared from week to week.
- The group might take time at the end of one session to look ahead and decide on the options they will cover in the next session. This could be time consuming.
- You might decide to do your personal preparation for the session (responding to the five questions), and when everyone comes together for the session, proceed on the basis of what topics interested people the most.

8. A FORMAT WITHIN EACH OPTION

Each of the options has four consistent elements: *Opening Essay, Beginning Conversation, The Teaching,* and *Group Response to the Teaching.*

- *Opening Essay by Phyllis Tickle* provides a way of receiving the essence and some detail concerning the main themes of that session. In a number of cases the paragraphs of the *Opening Essay* are numbered for easy reference in the options.
- *Beginning Conversation* provides an opportunity for people to think about the topic prior to seeing the DVD presentation. This "tilling of the soil" prior to the planting of seeds of learning creates in learners a deeper readiness for new ideas. It also makes it more likely that this new information will be connected to the body of knowledge that the learner already brings.
- *The Teaching* refers to the new input from the DVD as well as some text input. Within *The Teaching* you will receive direction about where to go on the DVD for the input and conversation relevant to that option. (Note that these are indicated by minutes and seconds [for example, *2:30-9:50*]. Note as well that there may be minor variations in the timing between different CD players and computers.) In some cases you will be directed to parts of the *Opening Essay.*
- *Group Response to the Teaching* provides experiential process for the group to follow after *The Teaching.* This is a time when the members of the group work with *The Teaching* and have the opportunity to integrate it into their own experience and frames of reference.

9. BEFORE THE SESSION

Each session opens with five questions for participants to consider as preparation for the session.

- We intend these questions to open in you some aspect of the topic being considered in the upcoming session. This may lead you to feel more confident when addressing this question in the group.
- Sometimes these questions are the same as ones raised in the context of the session. They provide opportunity for people to do some personal reflection prior to engaging in the group conversation on that topic.

10. CLOSING AS IF IT MATTERS

For each session there is a final option presenting a way of closing the session that emerges naturally from its content.

- It's important to close well. It's like a period at the end of a sentence. People leave the session ready for whatever comes next.
- Whether you use the closing option suggested or one of your own choosing, closing well matters.
- Another aspect of closing is evaluation. This is not included in an intentional way in the design of the sessions; however, evaluation is such a natural and satisfying thing to do that it could be included as part of the discipline of closing each session. It's as simple as taking time to respond to these questions:
  — What insights am I taking from this session?
  — What contributed to my learning?
  — What will I do differently as a result of my being here today?

POINTERS ON FACILITATION

1. Meeting Space

- Take time to prepare the space for the group. When people come into a space that has been prepared for them, they trust the hospitality, resulting in a willingness to bring the fullness of themselves into the conversation. Something as simple as playing recorded music as people arrive will contribute to this sense of "a space prepared for you."

- Think about how the space will encourage a spirit of reverence, intimacy and care. Will there be a table in the center of the circle where a candle can be lit each time the group meets? Is there room for other symbols that emerge from the group's life?

2. Opening

- In the opening session, take time to go around the circle and introduce yourselves in some way.

- Every time a group comes together again, it takes each member time to feel fully included. Some take longer than others. An important function of facilitation is to help this happen with ease, so people find themselves participating fully in the conversation as soon as possible. We designed these sessions with this in mind. Encouraging people to share in the activity proposed under *Beginning Conversation* is one way of supporting that feeling of inclusion.

- The ritual of opening might include the lighting of a candle, an opening prayer, the singing of a hymn where appropriate, and the naming of each person present.

3. Group Standards

- There are basic standards in group life that are helpful to name when a new group begins. Once they are named, you can always come back to them as a point of reference if necessary. Here are two basics:
  - Everything that is said in this group remains in the group. (confidentiality)
  - We will begin and end at the time agreed. (punctuality)

- Are there any others that you need to name as you begin? Sometimes standards emerge from the life of the group and need to be named when they become evident, otherwise they are just assumed.

SESSION | 1

EMERGENCE 101

ESSAY ONE BY PHYLLIS TICKLE

1. Most discussions, to be of any use to us at all, have to begin with some kind of common vocabulary or mutually-understood definitions. This discussion is certainly no different; and we must start with at least a few terms that are central to our over-all subject of Emergence Christianity.

2. Emergence Christianity is a global phenomenon, present in parts of both hemispheres and on every continent. In point of fact, as an operative and highly visible part of Christian expression, Emergence came last to the North American continent. Session One is going to refer to Emergence Christianity, then, as present in the *latinized world*, a term that is much more accurate and far less offensive than others like *Western World* or *First World*. *Latinized* refers to the cultures and countries who received Christianity through the Latin, as opposed to the Syriac or Greek language, or were colonized by those who had so received the faith, or were colonialized by those who had so received it.

3. The word *emergence* that keeps appearing everywhere these days originally had a far more focused and specific meaning than it presently enjoys in popular conversation. That is, Emergence (or Emergence Theory, to give it its full name) is a principle of the natural sciences. It studies and describes the non-hierarchal ways in which living creatures and their societies organize themselves, describing phenomena like the difference between a beehive and an anthill; the former is ruled by its queen and the latter by a communal operation in which no one is in charge and within which a queen is of use only as a breeder of more ants.

4. Wherever Emergence appears in nature, it always also involves a shift toward increased complexity. In fact, Emergence Theory as such was first discovered and formulated in the latter part of the 19th century in an attempt to understand why Darwin's principles of survival of the fittest and natural selection did not explain phenomena like human consciousness, let alone anthills. It is, then, the leap to an increased complexity, greater than that which could have been predicted from an organism's constituent parts, named both in the science lab and in sociology. The use of the term to name the huge lurch forward in complexity that characterizes both our times and the Church living and operating within them is, in other words, both a logical and a very informing choice, once we understand its history.

5. Emergence Christianity, while it names a new, more complex, and non-hierarchal form of Christianity, is not a monolith, any more than was the Protestantism that preceded it or the Roman Catholicism that preceded them both, or the monastic and episcopal Christianity that preceded all three of them. No one ever thought that all presentations of Protestantism are the same, one with another. We recognize Lutherans as being distinct from Presbyterians and both of them as distinct from Methodists, even though we are equally comfortable calling each of them "Protestants." That is, we recognize their separateness while at the same time recognizing their shared sensibilities and defining principles.

6. In the exact same way, Emergence Christianity is frequently referred to as a conversation. That generalized, non-specific definition is a way of saying that, though there are several distinct expressions of Emergence, they nonetheless hold in common certain principles and characteristics. For the purposes of our discussion, then, we must recognize that there are emerging expressions of Emergence and there are emergent ones, missional expressions and neo-monastic ones. There is deep church and Fresh Expressions of Church. There are house churches and even cyber churches. There are also the hyphenateds—those who have Emergence DNA deeply rooted in them, but who yet wish to retain the corpus of their natal tradition. They originally referred to themselves as Presby-mergents or Luther-mergents or Metho-mergents or Angli-mergents, thus gaining for themselves their

unusual name. Now the hyphens have more or less disappeared, and the words appear un-hyphenated as Presbymergents or Luthermergents, Methomergents, or Anglimergents, the hyphen living on now more in memory than in print. There are also responses to Emergence Christianity like today's neo-Calvinism and accommodations to it like Alt Worship.

7. Session One presents the great upheavals that have occurred in Latinized Christian culture and Christianity. It will outline as well the periods—or progression of periods—that are internal to each of those turnings. In general and with a variance of no more than a decade or two, each of the 'Greats' follows this internal pattern.

8. First, there is that moment in which the new way of thinking and being seems, almost abruptly, to have arrived at last as the operative and dominant part of the general and public conversation about the way things are. Thus we refer to the Great Reformation as having begun on October 31, 1517, even though we know quite well that there were years and decades of events that led up to Luther and his 95 Theses. In the same way, observers seem content now to think that the Great Emergence will be dated in history from the events of 9/11. Whether that be true or not, we can safely say that there is that defining moment when we recognize we have shifted into a "new" world.

9. Shortly after we recognize that the ground has seriously shifted beneath us and a new day has dawned, we realize as well that those changes and shifts have been creeping up on us for a very long time. Actually, they have been more or less roaring up on us for about a hundred and fifty years. That period of 150 years is called by its colloquial name of *tick-up,* or in a much more dignified way, as the *peri-* as in the peri-Reformation or the peri-Emergence.

10. What that hundred and fifty years of *peri-* that precedes each upheaval does is simply to chip away, slowly but inevitably, at the bases of authority that had accrued since the last upheaval and had given stability to both the Church and the culture in which it functions. As a result, the first century or so after our recognition of a dramatic and pervasive new way of being is spent trying to answer a very fundamental question: Given this shift, where now is our authority?

11. Once that question is answered, there follows a period of approximately 250 years in which we all more or less agree where authority is lodged. We may not like the answer—in fact, more and more of us usually don't—but we all agree that that authority is *the* authority, for better or for worse. And then, having gone through the whole process, we come back to the fifteen decades of *peri-* and commence again to disestablish that which our recent ancestors had so painfully set in place.

BEFORE THE SESSION

Many participants like to come to the group conversation after considering individually some of the issues that will be raised. The following five reflective questions are intended to open your minds, memories and emotions regarding some aspects of this session's topic. Use the space provided here to note your reflections.

What kind of time are we living in as Christians?

What place does the Bible have today in your relationship with God? How is that different than when you were half your present age?

How do you feel about being in a time of such dramatic change both in the culture and in the church?

Looking at change through the long lens of history can be a consolation in a time of dramatic change. To what extent is that true for you?

What are the essential concerns of your life today that you want to be able to address in the context of membership in a faith community?

OPTION 1: BIG PICTURE

Beginning Conversation

Take time to introduce yourselves to one another both by name and by completing this stem: *The three words I would personally use to describe the spirit or zeitgeist of the time through which we are living are*

1.
2.
3.

The Teaching

Session 1 introduces the theme of Emergence that we explore in greater detail in Sessions 2-6. For this reason, in this session we paint the topic with broad strokes, establishing the overall topic and terminology used throughout the series. Phyllis Tickle's opening essay is helpful in this regard. Be sure to read it before going on. Listen to roughly *the first 12 and a half minutes* of Phyllis's presentation on the DVD up to the point when the moderator invites questions from group members.

Group Response to the Teaching

As a group, complete the following statements as a way of affirming your grasp of the broad strokes of Phyllis Tickle's teaching:

- The metaphor of Bishop Mark Dyer that represents the kind of time in which we find ourselves living as Christians is...

- A word that is used both within Christianity and within the culture to identify the historical era which began in about 1842 and for which the events of September 11, 2001 were a significant marker is...

- The length of time that seems to be a given between these great historical upheavals in the latinized part of the world: The name given to the last great upheaval in which Martin Luther played an essential role is...

- In confronting the power of Roman Catholicism, Luther challenged the authority of the curia, the papacy and the Magisterium and proposed a new authority which is represented in these two Latin words:

- Within the greater cycle of change there is another timeline that includes a one hundred and fifty year period during which the established authority is eroded. This period that Phyllis refers to colloquially as 'the great tick-up' is also identified by the four-letter prefix...

- Many individuals and communities of Christians in all denominations identify themselves as *emergents*, but at the same time desire to remain within the body of their own tradition. Because they adopt a hybrid name that includes both their denominational identity as well as their emergence identity they are known as...

- Phyllis reckons that it takes about 100 years in each larger historical cycle to answer the key question of...

- The rise of the nation state, the formation of a middle class, the birth of capitalism, and the arrival of Protestantism, all emerged from that period of European history which is known as the...

- These cycles of history can also be seen extending back before the birth of Christ through 500 years of Jewish history to the time of exile known as...

OPTION 2: HERE WE ARE AGAIN!

Beginning Conversation

From your perspective, what are the clearest trends in latinized Christianity today?

The Teaching

Phyllis Tickle is very clear about the patterns that repeat *every time* humanity goes through one of these "great" 500-year historical reconfigurations:

- *Every time* the dominant and challenged form of Christianity does not cease to be.
- *Every time* the expressions of the old way have to drop back and reconfigure to make space for new.
- *Every time* the faith itself spreads and grows both geographically and demographically.
- *Every time* there are many expressions of the thing that is emerging.
- *Every time* there is one resounding question to be answered, and it is always the same question: Where now is our authority?

Group Response to the Teaching

What evidence do you see, both locally and globally, that we are living through such a time as Phyllis is describing?

OPTION 3: THE CHURCH AS INSTITUTION

Beginning Conversation

If you were able to ask Phyllis a question about what she has presented so far, what would it be?

The Teaching

Play the DVD from where you left off at around 13 minutes to 24:45-25:00, just before the moderator initiates a change in the conversation. Here group participants respond to Phyllis and ask clarifying questions. Notice that the issues raised by the group are all concerned with authority, order, hierarchy, rules, structure and church as institution.

Group Response to the Teaching

As you listened to the members of the small group and to Phyllis's responses to their questions, where did you feel particularly engaged; in other words, where did *their* concerns connect with *yours?*

OPTION 4: THE BIBLE AND EMERGENCE THEOLOGY

Beginning Conversation

In what way is the Bible a reflection of God's presence in human history?

The Teaching

Phyllis Tickle says on the DVD:

> Luther, when he said Sola Scriptura, shouldn't be blamed for what happened, namely Protestant inerrancy. There was no way that Luther could have foreseen Protestant inerrancy. What we mean by inerrancy is the belief that the Bible is absolutely, word for word, the word of God: historically accurate, consistent (if you don't read it!), and to be taken as a piece of history.

> I love emergence theology. I'm persuaded by so much of it. It's brilliant theology! One of the places I find it most appealing is that emergents will say, "Absolutely, the Bible is the word of God. It is God among us, but it is articulated in human speech and you cannot reduce God almighty to human speech articulation. It's worth to us is its actualness. To argue its historicity is to confine down to the limitations of our own intellect. How dare we! What is the arrogance that allows for that position!

Group Response to the Teaching

What is the distinction that Phyllis is making between the *inerrancy* of Scripture and the *actualness* of Scripture?

When has the Bible been "the word of God" for you?

OPTION 5: SPEAKING OF IMPACT

Beginning Conversation

What is the impact on you personally of what Phyllis Tickle is presenting in her teaching?

The Teaching

Play the remaining DVD segment from about 24:45-25:00 where the moderator asks, "How is this conversation impacting you personally?" Below we offer the five reactions of the members of the group, including Phyllis:

China, on finding context and building legacy:

> I'm in awe of how this conversation is adjusting me to my place, internally as well as in relation to my surroundings and to where I am in my life. It helps me see where I am in the course of history and why I'm feeling all the things I'm feeling and have felt for years. I've been figuring out what I'm going to impart to my children and what my legacy to them will be. What are they going to need to continue on, to understand these concepts about church and God, and to know how they are going to fit in?

Kim, on learning to listen to know who we should be:

> My gut is churning! What really did it was when you talked about those 'Emergence' churches saying, "Well, we may not be here in 10 years." I fall to my knees when I hear that because that's the question I keep coming back to in terms of the church I work for and love. It's very hard for me to think about 'not here' and yet there's a part of me that knows I need to be in this listening mode.
>
> China and I were in a group together not long ago and they began to talk about how they wanted to come together as a community. I said that I wanted to bring my teaching, but they replied, "No, we just want to be together!" So, I find myself having to listen a lot. It's hard because, as an American, I want everything now and I want to have the most numbers! That's what we've always been brought up to expect. We're looking at the whole and asking, "What are we and who should we be?"

James, on joining the search for new structure and authority:

> It makes me a little uncomfortable to hear all the talk about no authority and non-hierarchy. It's odd because I'm of the age that grew up on this non-hierarchal, no authority situation. My gut reaction is 'that's not healthy.' You need accountability. You need structure. We grow within these sort of confines; we are at our most free within confines, within structure of a certain type. But, I agree that maybe the old confines, the old structures weren't quite cutting it. Talking about what we're searching for makes sense.

Carolyn, on growing the conversation:

> *It's amazing to me to be sitting here having these conversations because it was in 1995 that my husband and I and others started asking many of these kind of questions. So, to think that 15 years later this is not only being talked about but it is really happening! I've come from a place of extreme confusion to a place where at least there's a whole bunch of us that are confused and talking about it.*

Phyllis, on acknowledging that it's out in the open:

> *Emergence theology excites me! What interests me most now is the interface with the institutional church. I'm 77. I'm not going to live to see the new authority established—the rules—the parameters. But it's now out in the general conversation in this country. We can now talk about it. We can defuse the fear. Fifteen years ago when I first began to talk this way, always my heart was broken when two or three folks would meet me after my presentation, either in the washroom or in the stair well and say, "O, thank God, I thought it was something we did!"*

Group Response to the Teaching

Which of these responses have resonance with your own reaction to what Phyllis Tickle is presenting?

What else would you say in response to the question, "How is all this talk of Emergence sitting with you?"

OPTION 6: THE WAY FORWARD

Beginning Conversation

Given the kind of time we are in, we need to be very clear about how we will be together while we live through this tumultuous time of social and religious upheaval and search for authority.

The Teaching

Here are ten key words drawn from the responses of the five group members in Option 5: *context, legacy, listening, humility, accountability, freedom, search, conversation, parameters* and *openness*. These words are more about the journey going forward than about the reality of emergence.

Group Response to the Teaching

What are key words to describe the kind of journey you think we are going on as we live through the Great Rummage Sale of the early 21st Century?

What are some of the "ways of being" that are required for such a journey?

OPTION 7: CLOSING AS IF IT MATTERS

Notice that, woven through the DVD presentation and perhaps through your own group discussion, there were strong exclamations by participants that showed that this conversation matters:

- *In a rummage sale you get rid of a lot of junk and you also find the treasures.*
- *My gut is churning!*
- *What am I going to impart to my children?*
- *My gut reaction is, "That's not healthy; you need authority!"*
- *There's a 300 pound gorilla in the living room.*
- *How do we know what to hold on to?*
- *I'm in awe...*
- *How dare we!*
- *It's amazing for me to be sitting here!*

In closing add your own expressions to this list.

Offer this prayer:

Holy One,
Known to us
    within the cycles of our living,
    through the rhythms of our history,
    from the sacred texts of our traditions,
    out of the concerns of our hearts, and
    in the insights of our minds,
May the reflections of our time together,
    stretch us into deepening awareness of your presence
    in the *then*, the *now* and the *to be* of your unfolding creation.
In the name of Jesus, the always of our lives.
Amen.

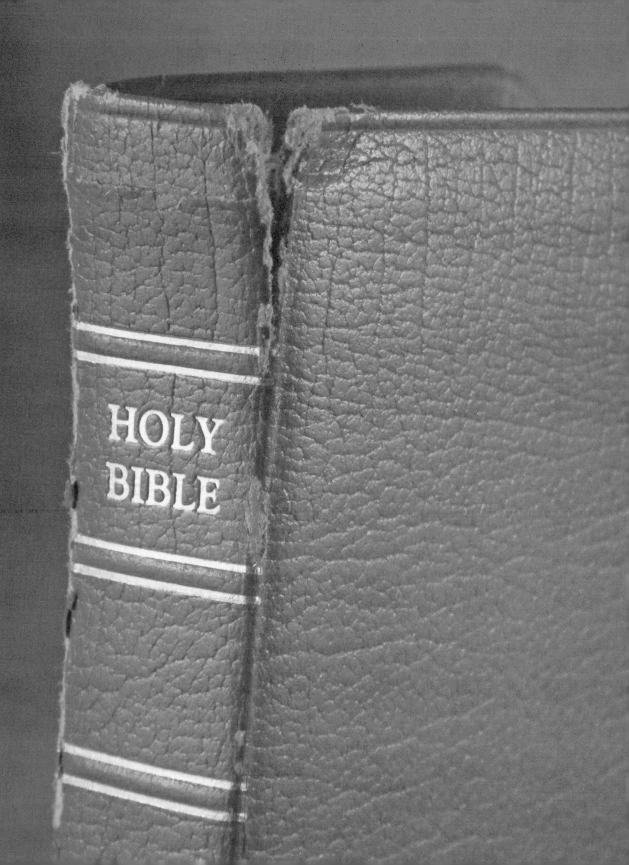

SESSION 2

WHERE NOW IS OUR AUTHORITY?

ESSAY TWO BY PHYLLIS TICKLE

1. As we approach any discussion of the peri-Emergence, we note, realistically and honestly, that the authority being disestablished over the past 15 decades (and even now), is the authority under which most Americans born prior to 1965 or 1970 have been shaped and reared. We are not, in other words, looking at the disestablishment of *an* authority, but at the disestablishment of *the* authority that has always been the guardian, instructor and counsellor for many—if not most—of us. Under those circumstances, the tenor of the conversation unavoidably shifts from a matter-of-fact overview of a neutral entity to a personal and sometimes threatening analysis of an unstoppable process. We would do well to remember that each of us is probably going to feel threatened (or at the very least discomforted) at one place or another, and that we have an obligation as participants in a guided conversation to respect empathetically not only our own pain or disquietude, but also that of all other participants.

2. That having been said, we need to acknowledge as well that the authority whose demise we are tracing is indeed that of *sola scriptura* and/or of its presentation as Protestant inerrancy. That demise raises not only the question of where now is our authority, but also the resultant one of what

then is the nature of Scripture's authority now. One cannot—indeed one should not—make blanket statements about Emergence Christianity and Emergence Christians as if they were a solid block of uniform theology and praxis, values and actions. That simply is not true and never could be. Both are composed of human beings, and human beings are ever and always different one from another, more often than not contentiously so. That should not stop us, however, from looking at what seems to be a consensus on some issues.

3. Emergence is in no way interested in, or inclined toward, disestablishing the authority of Scripture; rather it is dedicated to freeing that authority from *the constrictions of literalness*. As with the matter of how not to speak of God, so here too there is real fear among Emergence Christians that literalism is a form of apostasy. That is, trying to contain and confine God's word within the prison house of human logic and human comprehension is to act with an unconscionable degree of arrogance. It is to deny and destroy paradox, which is always an informing part of faith, and to demand of deity that God makes "sense" out of that part of God's Self which is Word. More to the point, at least at a daily level, it is still to function within a modernist or Enlightenment sensibility,

one that is reductionist, trying to possess reality by breaking it down systematically into its component parts, thereby destroying both the beauty and the power-bearing mystery of their articulation.

4. The word *myth* had little standing in modernism or Enlightenment thinking. It was, in fact, relegated by the Reformation and subsequent Enlightenment to naming that which was "nonfactual." Emergence Christianity, like the secular thinkers of the Great Emergence itself, is suspicious of "factual" per se and seeks to perceive the greater and instructive truth that is contained in story. It does not ask that that wisdom or instruction be always and ever understood in the same fashion by those who engage it; it asks instead—indeed argues—that such wisdom be always and ever true, whether correctly perceived or not.

5. The ancients—once more we find Emergence driving us back to the words and names of our forebears—the ancients had the word *mythos*, from which we obviously derive *myth*. But Emergence thinking, be it Christian or otherwise, now uses *mythos* as a way of speaking about the sweet and healing fragrance of meta-narrative. Mythos is the story of what a culture is or a people are. It contains, in other words, the soul of truth. Emergence and its citizens believe in the mythos, unfettered and always honored, more than in either historicity or non-contextualized fact. This leads Emergence Christians to be not literalists, but actualists. The best way to explain such a position, understandably enough, is to tell a story:

> Some twenty years ago now, I was addressing a Cathedral gathering on the historicity of the Virgin Birth. The Cathedral young people had served the evening's dinner and were busily scraping plates and doing general clean-up when I began the opening sections of the lecture I had come to give. The longer I talked, the more I noticed one youngster—no more than seventeen at the most—scraping more and more slowly until, at last, he gave up and took a back seat as part of the audience. When all the talking was done, he hung back until the last of the adults had left. He looked at me tentatively and, gaining courage, finally came up front and said, "May I ask you something?"
>
> "Certainly," I said. "What about?"
>
> "It's about that Virgin Birth thing," he said. "I don't understand."
>
> "What don't you understand," I asked, being myself rather curious by now because of his intensity and earnestness.
>
> "I don't understand," he said, "what their problem is," and he gestured toward the empty chairs the adults had just vacated.
>
> "What do you mean?" I asked him.
>
> "Well," he said, "it's just so beautiful that it has to be true whether it happened or not."

6. That one statement from a young Emergence teenager still stands for me—and always will—as a telling example of Emergence Christianity's understanding of Scripture and the nature of its authority. It is also a consoling one to call to mind at times like these.

BEFORE THE SESSION

Many participants like to come to the group conversation after considering individually some of the issues that will be raised. The following five reflective questions are intended to open your minds, memories and emotions regarding some aspects of this session's topic. Use the space provided here to note your reflections.

What place does the Bible have as an authority in your life?

When you think of the years between 1843 and 2001, what moments stand out for you and your family?

How do you practice compassion even to those with whom you have significant disagreement?

What do you like about this moment in history? How would you change it if you could?

What five things have the most authority in your life? How do you feel about that list?

OPTION 1: GETTING INTO THE MATERIAL

Beginning Conversation

As you begin this session, make sure that everyone has met and knows the names of group members. Take a moment to recall insights and questions from the first session that you are bringing forward into this session which will explore another facet of the Great Emergence.

The Teaching

In our first session Phyllis outlined for us the 500 year cycle that occurs consistently in our human experience that helps us to put a framework around what we are experiencing now in the Great Emergence. A quick review of this 500-year cycle:

1. 150 years: the *Peri* period, or as Phyllis sometimes refers to it, "The Great Tick-Up":
   - the widely accepted assumptions of the previous 250 year period begin to erode and crumble
   - disestablishment of the authority of the previous 250 years

2. A Transition Moment marked by some significant date in history
   - represents the cumulative effect of the previous 150 years and the start of the next phase of the cycle

3. 100 years: Dealing with the question: "Where now is our authority?"
   - establishes a new authority

4. 250 years: Now that the authority is established, a relatively stable period follows

In this session we look at some moments along the historical timeline as Phyllis offers reflection and guidance:

The Great Reformation

1: The Peri-Reformation (about 150 years)
   - 1380: Wycliffe begins the translation of the Bible into English.
   - 1390: Three armed Popes each contesting the Papacy engage in warfare in Southern Europe.
   - 1450: The fall of Constantinople and the flight of scholars back to Europe.
   - 1492: Columbus sails to lands on the other side of the Atlantic Ocean.

2: 1517: Transition Moment: The Peri-Reformation ends as Luther presents his 95 Theses.

3: For 100 years the latinized church deals once again with the question of authority and *sola scriptura* emerges as the Protestant authority distinct from the authority of the Roman Catholic Church.

4: For 250 years the church lives in relative stability within this new authority.

The Great Emergence

1. 1843: Peri-Emergence begins when Michael Faraday begins to define Field Theory and does pioneering work on electricity.

2: Transition Moment: September 11, 2001, the end of Peri-Emergence as the twin towers fall.

3: The 21st Century: a 100-year period in which we will focus once again on the question, "Where now is our authority?"

Having reviewed this historical framework, watch the DVD for Session 2.

Group Response to the Teaching

Note what stands out for you from Phyllis's opening essay, from the historical overview on page 31 and from the DVD. Now choose from the other options presented on the following pages.

OPTION 2: GOODBYE *SOLA SCRIPTURA*, HELLO MICAH 6:8

Beginning Conversation

In this session Phyllis focuses a lot of her teaching on the way that the 150 years of Peri-Emergence has seen the erosion of the principle of *sola scriptura*. She describes moments in this chipping away process, when *sola scriptura* as a defining principle of this era has been undermined and almost erased.

When in your life have you experienced a conflict between what you consider to be the requirements of Scripture and the prayerful wisdom of your own heart and mind?

The Teaching

In presenting her sociological overview of Peri-Emergence from 1843 to 2001, Phyllis reflects on specific moments in history that have a bearing on life within the Christian faith community in Europe and in North America.

First, Phyllis comes to the matter of slavery and the American Civil War:

> By the time you get to 1860 nobody thought it was very smart to own slaves. It's not efficient. It's an expensive way to do business. The problem from 1855 to 1860 when it was obvious we were going to go to war, the problem if you read the archives from every established denomination in the country except for the Brethren and Anglicans, the problem was not over whether slavery should be or not, the split was over, "could we not call it wrong?" That's because, while the Bible does not say you can buy somebody, the Bible clearly admits of slavery. Even if you get rid of the legal codes of Deuteronomy and Leviticus then you hit the New Testament with Philemon and Onesimus where there

> is slavery. The heart break for southern churchmen against north churchmen was, "Can we just not say it's wrong?" because the minute we say it's wrong then we have hit sola scriptura *and in many ways that was a more significant blow than even Darwin was at that time.*

In other words, those who had been involved in slavery and who continued to support it in principle whether they practised it or not, did not want to have to be in the position of condemning something as wrong which was clearly condoned by communities of faith in the Bible, the book whose inerrant authority was at the heart of their religious identity.

Second, when, in her historical overview of the Peri-Emergence, Phyllis comes to the matter of divorce and remarriage, she introduces an alternative Biblical principle for our consideration. She calls it Micah 6:8 theology. Here's how she speaks about it. Note that just prior to this excerpt, Phyllis described a situation involving a divorced woman and the way she was ostracized by her church community because she chose to leave a marriage in which she and her children were being abused and, in time, remarried a good and gentle man.

> What we get is the beginning of Micah 6:8 as theology. You hear Emergents talk about Micah 6:8 theology a lot. The passage from Micah says, "What does the Lord require of you, but to act justly, love mercy, and walk humbly with your God." And that's what she (the divorced woman) was doing and therefore as a church we're going to say that she's not an adulteress. Well it takes us a

while and those of us who remember the last century and its history remember that it's a big issue in the 60s and 70s. Can a divorced human being be ordained for heaven's sake! How scary is that! Can they even come in and hold positions of authority in the church? Well, we have eroded it and eroded it and eroded it so that now over half of us are divorced in one way or another. Did we pay a price? Yes. Is it Micah 6:8 theology? Yes, it is. But it's not sola scriptura because sola scriptura means, "You shall not do this!" and that's different from, "What does the Lord, thy God, require of you?" You can't have it both ways.

And third, Phyllis then takes us to the last playing piece of *sola scriptura*:

So what we have sociologically is the whole redefinition of what's right and what's wrong. Then we get to 1969. What we have done from slavery on is change the sociological interface of people with each other in terms of the established institutions as sola scriptura saw them. You get to 1969 and you get to Stonewall. And for the first time gay and lesbian, bisexual and transgendered people say, "Now it's our turn!"

The Bible is very clear about homosexuality. It's a fool who doesn't try to say what the Bible says. It does say it. So Micah 6:8 comes into play. What you've got now is close to 10% of our population falling within that category of gay and lesbian, bisexual and transgendered or some kind of mosaic. And it makes no sense to say these people are not fellow human beings with us. Micah 6:8 says you can't do that! Protestant inerrancy says, "Yes, you can." The fight right now is not about homosexuality. That is so over!

The fight right now is that when we say it's over, Protestant inerrancy is dead. It's the last playing piece in a deadly game and when we say by our actions, "That's yesterday's rules; we're all people together." Once we take that position, there's no place else to play the sola scriptura rules. Game over. It's the last piece still on the board. That's why it matters.

Group Response to the Teaching

Phyllis has presented what she refers to as a sociological cascade: a review of key historical themes and moments in the Peri-Emergence. Because she is describing events that were within our lifetime or within the lifetime of our parents and grandparents, we can bring a more personal perspective to the time being recalled.

What are your reactions to the insights that Phyllis has brought to us concerning the erosion of sola scriptura authority and the emergence of Micah 6:8 theology?

Phyllis has presented certain historical moments through the lens of the demise of *sola scriptura*. What other historical threads and themes might be offered as further evidence of the drama of the Peri-Emergence? Which ones of these touch most obviously on your life and the life of your family?

OPTION 3: THE PLACE OF COMPASSION IN A TIME OF CHANGE

Beginning Conversation

In her teaching Phyllis Tickle is presenting change of the most significant kind—a total re-ordering of the way we see things. Some people refer to it as a paradigm shift; that is, a change in perception as dramatic as ceasing to believe the earth is flat to knowing it is round. We don't need to go back 500 years to observe the impact of dramatic change in people's lives.

- When have you observed people dealing with the kind of change that requires them to see their world in a whole new way in order to be able to live in it?
- What place does compassion have in such a time? When have you felt compassion for people dealing with change? How have you expressed that compassion?

The Teaching

Phyllis says:

> We can't go through the upheaval that we call the Great Emergence without enormous compassion for our fellow Christians for whom this is a very painful thing. It will be very painful for all of us in one place or another, but it won't be the same pain in every place.

One of my favorite examples is from 1492 when Columbus sailed west on a flat earth. Nobody actually thought the earth was flat by 1492; it just didn't make any sense. What mattered was that the church still taught it was a flat earth and it was a stacked earth: hell—earth—heaven—and the universe beyond. Columbus sails west and doesn't fall off! At that point there's no way to accept what the church has said. You have to accept what he has just proved. This shouldn't be emotionally laden unless you look at some of the history. If I were a devout Christian in 1494 in London and I die and ascend as the faith teaches me in a round universe knowing that my Lord ascended 1500 years ago over here in the Holy Land in a flat universe, I'll never see my Lord again.

It's a heartbreak! It may seem foolish to us, but we should never say that something a fellow Christian is going through is foolish when it came from this kind of change.

Perhaps you will remember Phyllis's words of caution and care from her essay at the beginning of this session:

> We would do well to remember that each of us is probably going to feel threatened (or at the very least discomforted) at one place or another, and that we have an obligation as participants in a guided conversation to respect empathetically not only our own pain or disquietude, but also that of all other participants.

In responding to Phyllis, Kim says the following:

I'm really struck by your talking about the inerrancy of the Bible really beginning to die with the whole slavery issue. I've had a really difficult time understanding people who believe in the inerrancy of the Bible and what they have to say about the whole gay issue, partly because I have such good friends who are gay and I know their stories and I know their heartache. [Your analysis] helps me understand why that is so important to the people for whom it is important and I think there's a bit of grace for me in this conversation—to get to that. The bottom line for me is I have a little bit more love for the people for whom this is a really difficult issue.

And China says of her father:

I just think of my father who just could not to his dying day let go of sola scriptura *at all. So I feel more compassion for him after what you say, Phyllis.*

Group Response to the Teaching

What kind of changes are people experiencing in the second decade of the 21st Century that demand a high degree of compassion?

Do you have personal examples of the kind of compassionate response that is growing in Kim and China as they understand in a new way how scriptural authority plays into the lives of other people, even members of their own families?

What is your practice of compassion?

OPTION 4: IMPLICATIONS, UPON FINDING OURSELVES AT THIS EDGE

Beginning Conversation

The *edge* is the beginning of the 100 years that it will take to resolve the question: What now is our authority? Each of the members of the group meeting with Phyllis struggled with what it means for them personally to be at that point in history. Just before you read those four expressions, talk together about what it is like for you to be just beyond 150 years of Peri-Emergence and immersed in this profound question concerning authority.

The Teaching

Read these four reflections on change by the four group members.

China, on thinking multi-dimensionally:

What I see is something moving from two-dimensional to three-dimensional. When we're talking sola scriptura—*it's black and white, it's two-dimensional. We are putting flesh on it more and more and more to the point that it just can't exist the way that it has existed. It just doesn't hold up. What we are creating is corporal— three-dimensional—and, hopefully, four-dimensional when God breathes the Spirit of God into it. I see it taking shape!*

Carolyn, on wondering about the new authority

The idea of sola scriptura *not being the authority is still a little mind boggling to me because even in different traditions when scripture is looked at differently—from literal interpretation to more imaginative interpretation—we might still say quite casually, "O, sola scriptura" even though we differ on what we actually mean by it. So then, my question is, What does it look like if that isn't the authority?*

Kim, on listening to one another in love:

It all comes back to dialogue and to be in a position where we are trying to understand the other in love. I think that's what I've loved about being Anglican all this time. We're at least trying to understand what somebody else has in their mind. I think if we come to that maybe then we can help each other move through what is, to whatever is emerging.

James, on acknowledging the Processes of change:

I'm not convinced that we're going to get away from Bible-olatry. I could see us being as fundamental about our new interpretation, our new understanding, our new integration of the Bible as the previous generation that we think were off the mark. I think we're going to struggle with that all over again and, as much as we might all believe in our own interpretation and say, "Well, what matters more is love. Love 'em; and if they're doing it in love, it's fine." Than making that dogmatic and hating the people who don't agree with us.

Phyllis, in response to James:

Of course. We've already started that process and each of the 500 year periods—each of the new forms that emerged—did the same thing until they became rigid again.

Group Response to the Teaching

What is the impact of all of this on your own faith community? Perhaps Phyllis's teaching is providing you with some ways of understanding what's going on for you and for the others in your congregation. Given what you have read and seen in this session, what things might you as a community begin to do, or do differently? You might use the kind of wording used above:

- wondering about the new authority
- thinking multi-dimensionally
- listening to one another in love
- acknowledging the processes of change

OPTION 5: CLOSING AS IF IT MATTERS

Designate half the group A and the other half B. Read Micah 6:6-8 responsively, as shown here:

Micah 6:6-8

A.   With what shall I come before the Lord, and bow myself before God on high?

B.   Shall I come before God with burnt offerings, with calves a year old?

A.   Will the Lord be pleased with thousands of rams, with tens of thousands of rivers of oil?

B.   Shall I give my firstborn for my transgression, the fruit of my body for the sin of my soul?'

A.   God has told you, O mortal, what is good;

B.   and what does the Lord require of you

All: but to do justice, and to love kindness, and to walk humbly with your God?

One: May it be so.

SESSION | 3

THE 20ᵀᴴ CENTURY AND EMERGENCE

ESSAY THREE BY PHYLLIS TICKLE

1. As we move into our third session together, we must remind ourselves that what we are doing here is simply an overview of Emergence, no more and no less. Like all overviews, this one should—and hopefully will—invite as many questions as it attempts to answer.

2. By my own count, there are at least 44 distinct events, inventions and discoveries that have led us, since 1842/3, to the Great Emergence and to the Emergence Christianity that is a component of it. Some observers, of course, may have even longer lists. In any case, there is no way, nor any need, for us to consider all of them here. Instead, we have used the principle of sociological cascades and the time unit of decades to expose some ideas and discoveries that, occurring within the peri-Emergence, affected theology and the authority of *sola scriptura*. Before we leave the peri-Emergence, however, we need to look as well at examples of purely commercial "things" that also occurred within the peri-Emergence, but that affected the church and the business of how we "do church" more directly than they affected theology or doctrine, at least in some immediately obvious way.

3. **The Second World War,** like most wars in history, brought with it not only unspeakable destruction and heartbreak, but also significant advances in medicine, technology and popular access to knowledge. None of these has more subtly insinuated itself into church than has television. From the moment that old soldier, General Douglas MacArthur, chose not to die, but to fade away on the still grainy and rare screens of America in the spring of 1951, we were hooked. We had access to "the real thing," to the immediacy of simultaneous seeing and hearing, to the "authority" of the man himself. He was speaking to us here, now, in our own homes. He was not there, but here; not an abstraction, but a genius whom we could "know" without mediation. The truly important thing for church, though, was that in that same year of 1951, a bishop named Fulton Sheen made the same move from abstraction to absolute presence, from out there somewhere to in here with us.

4. What Bishop Sheen opened up, of course, was first the whole world of **televangelism**. Other permutations like the "live church via TV" phenomenon would come later, but the televangelists alone were enough to disenchant, if not outright disgust, millions of us. Still other millions found that going to church electronically was much easier—and just as good, supposedly—as getting dressed on Sunday. Going somewhere to church began to seem quaint or just plain old-fashioned and unnecessary for many of us.

5. Beyond all of that and whether anybody intended it or not, we suddenly were forced to realize that there was a whole panoply of theological ideas and pastoral opinions and group ways of worship out there. Given such an obvious variety of well-presented and skillfully marketed ways of doing and believing, which were we to accept as the "right" way or the "correct" set of beliefs or position? Obviously, there were too many of them for anybody to know, really, and so many that perhaps none was to be held wholeheartedly and without some reservations. **Electronic church** along with electronic pastors had been born. Some would even say that so, too, had electronic god. Whether that be true or not, certainly the presentations and enactments of life events like those "touched by an angel" became a compelling folk theology.

6. In much the same way, by 1989, Joseph Campbell, with the management and collaboration of that greatest of communicators, Bill Moyers, was to open our awareness to the similarities embedded in all religions. In that exchange, we would discover more than ecumenism and a discomfort with religious exclusivity and particularity. We would discover—or some observers would discover in us—the fact that information which comes in to us as entertainment and while we are in the comfort and safety of domestic space, comes in more subtly, less vetted and more credibly than does that which is doled out by a man in an elevated box in front of which we, his hearers, sit rooted to the floor in hard pews and wearing neckties or high-heels. Welcome to *everything!*

7. Along the same lines and almost lost in its own obviousness—hidden in plain sight, so to speak—was the coming of the **Sony Walkman** in 1979. It had been preceded, obviously, by things like the phonograph and the 8-Track, just as television had been preceded by the radio, but there was a significant difference here between an 8-track and a Walkman. Now one could plug the music into one's own ears and create a moving, portable environment of really good, brilliantly performed music. The early Walkman was as nothing, of course, compared to what was to come, but it was a beginning. Now music could be "incarnational" and even incarnated, could be danced to wherever one was, jived too, even, with clicking fingers, bobbing heads and hip-hopping feet.

8. In the 19th and early 20th centuries, good music—real music—was the privilege of the wealthy and/or to some extent, of the urbanized. Either way, it certainly could not be carried about upon one's person, much less individualized and particularized. No, up until 1979, good music for ordinary folk was most readily found in cathedrals and churches where it might at times offer transcendence, but not repeatable and incarnational participation. The problem in all of this is that church—at least established church—forgot to make note of the change. It persisted, instead—even to this very day—in offering performance or performed music that is non-participatory in every way. Emergence Christian gatherings, on the other hand, make no such mistake.

9. And so it goes. The point here in looking at an example or two of the very mundane shaping the sacred is that each of us who cares about the Church and Faith has need of a clear mind and a set of equally clear eyes. To argue or distress ourselves about whether we like or even approve of what has happened and continues to happen in our time is a waste of time as well as of emotional energy and focus. It is, in fact, rather like disapproving because the sun insists on getting up each morning earlier than we wish to wake up. The sun will do as it must, with or without our approval. Better, then, to put our minds to understanding the ways of the sun, to a consideration of the best ways of greeting it, of enjoying its benefits and of celebrating its power and magnificence…which, when all is said and done, is exactly what we are trying to do here in our conversation with one another.

BEFORE THE SESSION

Many participants like to come to the group conversation after considering individually some of the issues that will be raised. The following five reflective questions are intended to open your minds, memories and emotions regarding some aspects of this session's topic. Use the space provided here to note your reflections.

In what way is your relationship to the Bible different from your parents and your grandparents?

What big questions are you struggling with at this time in your life? To what extent are those questions big as a result of your social context rather than personal circumstances?

Given that the Bible has come to us as a result of the accidents of history, the political ambitions of rulers, the spiritual insights of writers and the convictions of the faithful inspired, what place does it hold in your life?

What has been the most influential public event of your lifetime? What influence did that event have on the emerging story of our time?

Engaging with story is one very significant way that we make sense of our lives both individually and collectively. What place does story have in your life and in your way of making meaning?

OPTION 1: THE BIBLE AND PERI-EMERGENCE: FROM SCHWEITZER TO THE JESUS SEMINARS

Beginning Conversation

In what way is your relationship to the Bible different from that of your parents and your grandparents?

The Teaching

Listen to Phyllis Tickle on the DVD speaking about Albert Schweitzer and the new understandings of the Bible that his work ushered into the 20th Century (approximately the first 9 minutes of Session 3).

Notes on Schweitzer:

- Albert Schweitzer (14 January 1875–4 September 1965) was a Franco-German theologian, organist, philosopher, physician and medical missionary.
- As a music scholar and organist he studied the music of Bach and influenced the organ reform movement.
- In a flash of insight he realized that the Jesus of Nazareth and the Christ of history are not the same person. His book, *The Quest for the Historical Jesus*, published in 1906, develops this insight.
- He realized that there was no way to know who Jesus of Nazareth really was.
- Given that he could not know who Jesus really was, he dedicated his life to live the way that he knew the Christ of history would have him live.
- Schweitzer went on to found and sustain a hospital in Lambarene, now in Gabon, in west central Africa.
- In 1952 he received the Nobel Peace Prize for his philosophy, *Reverence for Life*.

- Schweitzer articulates a major question of the Peri-Emergence: *What is the historical Jesus?*

(Source: Wikipedia, the free encyclopedia, *http://en.wikipedia.org/wiki/Albert_Schweitzer*)

Phyllis links Schweitzer to Nag Hammadi:

There's a straight line from that question and that answer ("No, I can never know who Jesus of Nazareth was. It's not given to me to know that. All I can know is the Christ of history and try to live as he would have me live.") all the way to 1945 and Nag Hammadi and the discovery there of the library that contained things that we didn't even know were extant.

Notes on Nag Hammadi:

- The Nag Hammadi Library, a collection of thirteen ancient codices containing over fifty texts, was discovered in upper Egypt in 1945.
- This immensely important discovery includes a large number of primary Gnostic scriptures, texts once thought to have been entirely destroyed during the early Christian struggle to define orthodoxy.
- This includes scriptures such as the *Gospel of Thomas*, the *Gospel of Philip* and the *Gospel of Truth*.
- The discovery and translation of the Nag Hammadi library, completed in the 1970s, has provided impetus to a major re-evaluation of early Christian history and the nature of Gnosticism.

Notes on Gnosticism:

- In the first century CE the term *Gnostic* denoted one group within the diverse Christian community.
- The *Gnostics* identified themselves by claiming not only a belief in Christ and his message, but a special experience of the divine.
- They asserted that this experience or *gnosis* was the mark of the true followers of Christ.
- In the first 150 years of Christianity, no single acceptable format of Christian thought had yet been defined. During this formative period. Gnosticism was one of many expressions within the new religion.
- The tide of history turned against Gnosticism in the middle of the 2nd century.
- Gnosticism's emphasis on personal experience, its continuing revelations and production of new scripture and its asceticism were all met with increasing suspicion.
- The first attacks on Gnosticism as heresy were published in 180 CE and continued with increasing vehemence throughout the next century.
- By the end of the 4th century, the struggle was over, and Gnosticism as a Christian tradition was largely eradicated, its remaining teachers ostracized and its sacred books destroyed. Or at least so it seemed until the mid-20th century.

(Source: The Gnostic Society Library:
An Introduction to Gnosticism
and The Nag Hammadi Library,
http://www.gnosis.org/naghamm/nhlintro.html)

Phyllis continues:

And then to Qumran in 1947…

Notes on Qumran:

- Qumran is a ruin from the days of the Second Temple on the northwest shore of the Dead Sea.
- It became famous since 1947 when a number of ancient manuscripts were found in nearby caves. These manuscripts are now known as the Dead Sea Scrolls.
- Since the discovery from 1947 to 1956 of nearly 900 scrolls in various conditions, mostly written on parchment, with others on papyrus, extensive excavations of the settlement have been undertaken.
- Many scholars believe the location to have been home to a Jewish sect, the Essenes.
- The scrolls were found in a series of eleven caves around the settlement, some accessible only through the settlement.
- Some scholars have claimed that the caves were the permanent libraries of the sect, due to the presence of the remains of a shelving system. Other scholars believe that some caves also served as domestic shelters for those living in the area.
- Many of the texts found in the caves appear to represent widely accepted Jewish beliefs and practices, while other texts appear to speak of divergent, unique or minority interpretations and practices.
- Most of the scrolls seem to have been hidden in the caves during the turmoil of the First Jewish Revolt, 67-70 CE, though some of them may have been deposited earlier.

(Source: Wikipedia, the free encyclopedia,
http://en.wikipedia.org/wiki/Qumran)

Phyllis then leads us into the question of the closing of the Canon of Scripture.

Notes on the Canon:
- A Biblical canon—or canon of scripture—is a list of books considered to be authoritative as scripture by a particular religious community.
- The term itself was first coined by Christians, but the idea is found in Jewish sources.
- The canonical books have been developed through debate and agreement by the religious authorities of their respective faiths.
- Believers consider these canonical books to be inspired by God or to express the authoritative history of the relationship between God and God's people.
- Books, such as the Jewish-Christian Gospels, excluded from the canon are considered non-canonical, but many disputed books considered non-canonical or even apocryphal by some are considered biblical apocrypha or fully canonical by others.
- There are differences between the Jewish and Christian biblical canons, and between the canons of different Christian denominations. The differing criteria and processes of canonization dictate what the communities regard as the inspired books.

(Source: Wikipedia, the free encyclopedia, *http://en.wikipedia.org/wiki/Biblical_canon*)

Phyllis on the Canon of Scripture:

The question then is "Why is the Canon closed? Why should the Canon be closed? Who said the Canon is closed?" It is entirely possible that the canonical Gospels and maybe the first two chapters of Acts really are the New Testament and we need to look again at some of these letters and writings. Maybe they were just that. Maybe they weren't the inspired word of God. Maybe if Nicaea had heard more it wouldn't have done this.

Notes on Nicaea:
- The First Council of Nicaea was a council of Christian bishops convened in Nicaea in present-day Turkey by the Roman Emperor Constantine I in A.D. 325.
- The Council was the first effort to attain consensus in the church through an assembly representing all of Christendom.
- Its main accomplishments were settlement of the Christological issue of the relationship of Jesus to God the Father, the construction of the first part of the Nicene Creed, settling the calculation of the date of Easter and the official announcement of early canon law.

Phyllis again:

And then, of course, it led to alternate editions of the Bible. It led us very quickly to the awareness that the last part of Mark as we have it in The King James Bible and everything since probably wasn't there originally; it was a tie-on later. And so we get the birth of textual criticism. And textual criticism begins to raise all kinds of intellectual and perfectly valid questions about the Canon and you get to these questions: What is Canon? How do we know? How can you put your total faith in a document that doesn't even seem to be agreed upon in terms of what it is?

And finally Phyllis on the Jesus Seminars:

When you get beyond Nag Hammadi and Qumran you get that wonderful thing called the Jesus Seminars in the 1980's...

Phyllis description of the process used in discernment by the scholars of the Jesus Seminars is so thorough on the DVD that there is no need to repeat it here. It's important, however to be familiar with it because it marks the end of the overview of textual criticism that Phyllis has offered beginning with Schweitzer's great insight in the first decade of the century.

Group Response to the Teaching

What are the key insights you have as a result of Phyllis's teaching in this first portion of Session 3 on the DVD?

Things about the Bible that seemed set in stone, unquestionable, even sacred in another age have been dislodged by events of the 20th Century. We are by no means at the end of that process. It was all part of the displacement of an authority by which we have lived since the time of the Protestant Reformation. What questions or wonderings have been generated in you as a result of this section of teaching? What feelings do you have about it all?

It's hard not to be aroused and curious in the face of such energetic teaching. What topics or issues do you intend to pursue further as a result of Phyllis's teaching in this section?

OPTION 2: HOW CULTURE CHANGES THE WAY WE DO CHURCH

Beginning Conversation

In her opening essay Phyllis Tickle writes:

> To argue or distress ourselves about whether we like or even approve of what has happened and continues to happen in our time is a waste of time as well as of emotional energy and focus. It is, in fact, rather like disapproving because the sun insists on getting up each morning earlier than we wish to wake up. The sun will do as it must, with or without our approval. Better, then, to put our minds to understanding the ways of the sun, to a consideration of the best ways of greeting it, of enjoying its benefits and of celebrating its power and magnificence…which, when all is said and done, is exactly what we are trying to do here in our conversation with one another.

The Teaching

If you haven't already, read Phyllis's opening essay for this session.

Group Response to the Teaching

There are so many ways that we could name how "the mundane has shaped the sacred" since 1940. Phyllis offers five key influences:
- The Second World War
- Televangelism
- Electronic Church
- Joseph Campbell and Bill Moyers
- Sony Walkman 1979

What other commercial "things" would you name that occurred within the peri-Emergence, that affected "church" and the business of how we do it more directly than they affected theology or doctrine, at least in some immediately obvious way. What exactly was the affect of those things on how we do church?

In what ways is your church, either locally, regionally or nationally, living in a relationship of mutual creativity with the culture of which it is both a part and apart?

Where would you and the other members of the group put yourselves on this scale about your relationship with change:

1	2	3	4	5	6	7	8	9	10

over my dead body   Well, if I have to...   It's an unavoidable   Change helps   The more change,
but just this once   fact of life   me grow   the better!

OPTION 3: JUST ONE DECADE!

Beginning Conversation

Choose one decade of your life and name the moments of those 10 years that give it significance in the human journey, both sacred and secular.

The Teaching

In her teaching on this DVD, Phyllis Tickle makes the point that some decades are more seminal in advancing the kind of change that we are addressing in this series. The 1960s was one such decade. We are familiar with that one because many of us alive today lived through that decade and remember it well. We are not so familiar with the first decade of the twentieth century.

You have heard Phyllis speaking about the emergence of textual criticism beginning with Albert Schweitzer and ending with the Jesus Seminars. Now continue her journey through that first decade of the last century.

Watch the next portion os of Session 3 on the DVD (beginning at approximately 9:00 and ending around 25:15).

Group Response to the Teaching

Without going into scientific detail, talk about the contribution that Einstein (1879–1955) made to the Peri-Emergence that Phyllis is presenting. William Seymour (1870–1922) may not be as familiar a name as Einstein, yet his contribution to the birth of Pentecostalism is immense. What was new information for you from Phyllis's telling of the story?

The arrival of the Model T in 1908 (presented in Option 4) marks the fourth seminal contribution of the 1900–1910 decade to the process of emergence, both cultural and religious, that Phyllis is describing:

- Albert Schweitzer publishes *Search for the Historical Jesus* in 1906.
- Albert Einstein writes four key scientific papers in 1905.
- William Seymour and the Birth of Pentecostalism begins in 1906.
- The Model T Ford arrives in 1908.

Stop for a moment and note together how different the story of emergence would have been without the contributions of these people and events.

OPTION 4: IT'S ALL ABOUT HESTIA!

Beginning Conversation

Can you believe that it's just over 100 years since the first Model T rolled off the assembly line of the Ford Motor Company? How has your life and the lives of people in your family been significantly shaped by that one technological event?

The Teaching

Watch the third portion of Session 3 on the DVD (beginning at approximately 25:15 and ending around 29:15-30:00).

Phyllis, on the impact of the Model T Ford (also called the *Flivver* and the *Tin Lizzie*), says:

> *In 1908 the coming of the Tin Lizzie allows us to begin to be mobile and as it does the first thing that happens is that we don't go to the village church anymore. We begin to go on a picnic on a Sunday with the children. We don't go to Grandma's house for Sunday lunch. We begin to move away from the village. Grandma has this influence and the village has this influence. The Model T cuts us free of the village. It cuts us free of Grandma and you can watch the progression from Sabbath to Lord's Day to Sunday to Day Off to "Let's do it on Saturday night." So Sabbath is eroded. Grandma is eroded. It's highly important although it sounds so superficial.*

In response to Phyllis's teaching, Kim says:

> *I'm just thinking about not going to Grandma's house anymore and about how much I'm constantly thinking about what the families with children are dealing with in today's culture. I hear from youth all the time about how incredibly over-scheduled they are, about how much homework they have and how much is expected of them. I tell them that college is going to feel like fun when they get there because they're not going to have nearly as much to do. I feel like our society has just piled so much on us that we're expected to do. We don't have that Sunday dinner, sit on the porch and just talk, glass of iced tea or whatever time anymore. I wonder where that's going in our culture and how that is going to affect who we are as church and what people are looking for. I think that's one of the reasons why people are looking for community in our church setting.*

And China adds:

> *It's about Hestia, the Goddess of Hearth and Home. There's no longer Hestia, stoking the fire, keeping the fire alive at home. Hestia has left the nest and there's a vacuum there. You just can't go on without her. Something has to fill that; we're looking for that everywhere.*

And Kim concludes:

That's one of the things that came out of 9/11 and out of the economic crunch of the last couple of years. So many people I've talked to have said, "We're re-thinking everything. We're re-thinking what's important; what we need to buy, what Christmas needs to be." I think that kind of tragedy brings us up short to re-think our lives. I wonder at what point people are going to say, "We need to reclaim that."

Group Response to the Teaching
What kind of things are you experiencing that are related to the social analysis offered by Phyllis, Kim and China?

Kim uses the word *re-thinking* to describe the kind of activity that many churches are involved in today. What kind of re-thinking are you involved in with your faith community? Have you been bold enough in your consideration of new ways of being in ministry in the 21st Century? What more might be needed?

OPTION 5: TELLING THE STORY; LISTENING TO SPIRIT

Beginning Conversation

What place does storytelling have in your life right now?

The Teaching

Phyllis says:

> One of the great characteristics of Emergence Christianity is its narrative. Tell us the story, don't tell us the doctrine. Don't tell us the creed. Tell us the story! Because unless Fisher Price made a toy out of it, they don't know the story. Daniel in the Lion's Den we got; Noah and the Flood we got, but we don't know which comes first and where they fit.

Carolyn reflects on two different ways of approaching the Bible:

> The holistic view is very different from the "Let's pick apart each particular verse and see how many times this word is used or that word is used…" It's about connecting the dots, instead of looking at each little dot. Let's look at all the dots and see what the picture is when we connect them all.

Kim adds:

> Through using Godly Play, not only with children but also with adults, people know these Bible stories, but they know them in a stance of awe and wondering and an ability to be open-hearted to what they don't understand or what doesn't seem quite right. In our worship we say together, "Hear what the Spirit is saying to us." I've been doing more and more listening to what the Spirit is saying right now, in this moment. I want, like a lot of people, to be more in touch with the inspiration of the Bible. I've found that one of the ways for me to be more open is to use a spiritual practice like centring prayer or Lectio Divina in which I can centre down and open myself to what God might be telling me.

Group Response to the Teaching

To what extent are you an "emergent Christian" in the way that Phyllis speaks about it with regard to the Bible?

The three excerpts from the teaching DVD hint at just a few of the many ways of building relationship with the Bible:
- soaking in the stories as they are read or told
- understanding the context in which a story was written
- following a story through many chapters and perhaps more than one book
- appreciating the meaning and significance of each word
- receiving and enjoying the text as an interconnected, unbroken whole
- wondering about the aspects of a story that are unstated in the text
- praying with the text to receive spiritual insights
- meditating on specific words or phrases
- having conversation in small groups about the meanings you find in the text
- stepping into the lives of people in the text through drama and storytelling

OPTION 6: CLOSING AS IF IT MATTERS

What kind of relationship would you like to have with the Bible at this time in your life?

What activities appeal to you as a way of building that new relationship?

Take a moment in closing to sit quietly—perhaps with eyes closed—and reflect on all that has claimed your attention, your head and heart, your creative spirit and your vision in this time together.

Choose just one word or phrase to represent what you are taking with you from this session.

Go around the circle with each person saying their name and what it is they are taking with them, like this:

I am _____, and from this session I am taking _____
_____.

Conclude with this prayer:

Holy One,
Take our names and hold them in
your care,
Take our insights and scatter them like
seeds into your unfolding creation,
Take our gratitude and stretch it into
loving intention for the days until
we meet again.
Amen.

SESSION | 4

GIFTS FROM OTHER TIMES

ESSAY FOUR BY PHYLLIS TICKLE

1. One of the less-frequently discussed but more fascinating patterns of our cultural and ecclesial cycling is the fact that each new presentation of the faith—in our case, Emergence Christianity—always jumps back over the entire, previous half a millennium in order to re-consider what had been good and worthy in the Christianity of that earlier time. The question, whether self-awaredly raised or not, is one of sorting out what got thrown away to discover what should have been kept, maybe even what should be restored to its proper place of honor. Emergence Christianity certainly has done and is doing that very thing with insistence and increasing obviousness. That is to say that many of the ways in which Emergence Christianity is diverging from Protestant or Roman Christianity are, in point of fact, a re-assertion and re-adoption of ideas, both in theology and in praxis, that were normative prior to the Great Schism, but were abandoned or scorned by the Roman Christianity that came as a result of it. To appreciate Emergence Christianity at all, we must look at three or four of these restored castaways.

2. At a most obvious and perhaps less deliberated level, Emergence Christianity has restored and/or taken (depending on one's point of view) from Orthodoxy, a major hallmark of its mode of worship. That is, incarnational worship is a central and defining characteristic of Emergence; but we must understand what that term means in today's context.

3. *Incarnational*, as it is generally used by Protestant and Roman Christians, refers to the assuming of bodily form by the Godhead in the person of Jesus of Nazareth. For Emergence Christians, that certainly is true; but *incarnational worship* or the variants thereof means something else as well, something more. It means the movement or transposition of the worship experience deeply into the physical life of the worshiper. Incarnational worship is to "feel" in every part of the worshiper's body the totality of the experience. It is to know in one's flesh that the whole of one's creatureliness is worshiping simultaneously and completely. Accordingly, we find in Emergence worship the heavy use of icons, most as rendered in the Greek or Orthodox manner. There is, as a rule, substantial movement, including liturgical dance, just as there is not infrequently the use of color and costume of an Eastern aesthetic. Perhaps more interestingly—and perhaps just as informatively—there is a return to the use of "sweet bread" for the Eucharist and sometimes even of chocolate. The use of sweet bread instead of unleavened bread was a major (albeit to us now a somewhat superficial) point of dissension in the

Great Schism. And as for the chocolate, Nadia Boltz-Webber, a major leader within Luthermergence in the USA, is fond of saying, "Nothing says *resurrection* like chocolate, Baby," which pretty much sums the whole thing up in one short sentence.

4. At a headier level, we must consider the return of the *filioque*. Long buried—a thousand years buried, in point of fact—*filioque* is Latin for "and from the Son." Minor as that may seem to us nowadays, it was a major sticking point between east and west in the Great Schism. The argument had to do with the west's (i.e., Roman Christianity's) insistence that the Holy Spirit was descended from God, the Father *and from God, the Son* (that is, *filioque*). The eastern or Orthodox position contended instead that *both the Holy Spirit and the Son* descended from the Father. The former position, which has informed the Roman and Protestant presentations of the faith for a thousand years, is a kind of upside-down isosceles triangle standing on its point. The latter and Orthodox understanding gives us that same isosceles triangle, but standing this time firmly on its base.

5. Emergence Christianity is deeply, radically Trinitarian, denying the *filioque* and asserting instead the operative presence of a co-equal, co-eternal Trinity. Emergence defines this relationship by the Greek word *perichoresis*. It is the ancient word from which we get *choreography*; but before someone scorns it as just too esoteric to remember, one needs to know that it is on the lips and in the thinking of far more ordinary Emergence Christians than not. What *perichoresis*

names is the dance of the blue, red and yellow flames in the dancing fire, all of them blending one into the other, all of them separate but inseparable, distinguishable but indistinguishable, all of them depending upon and from one another. The result of this re-adoption is, as we have said, a radical trinitarianism.

6. Perhaps one last characteristic of pre-Great Schism theology that has been adopted and adapted by Emergence should be mentioned here before we conclude our study. Peter Rollins, a major Emergence theologian, wrote some few years ago a book entitled *How (Not) To Speak of God*. While such may sound clever or flip, nothing could be farther from the truth. In eastern or Orthodox Christianity there is what is called *apophatic* theology. As a way of conceptualizing God, it has a near-kin cousin in Roman theology called the *via negative,* though the two are not precisely identical. Emergence is apophatic. That is, Emergence in general holds that there is an intolerable and highly dangerous human arrogance in any attempt to describe what God is by means of human language. Better to say what God is not—as in "God is not subject to human description"—than to try to say, "God is good," with the full knowledge that we human beings have not an articulatible clue about what "good" is. Better to say that God is neither good nor not good, but is, and is beyond such knowing. Again, the subtleties are exquisite as well as informing.

BEFORE THE SESSION

Many participants like to come to the group conversation after considering individually some of the issues that will be raised. The following five reflective questions are intended to open your minds, memories and emotions regarding some aspects of this session's topic. Use the space provided here to note your reflections.

When have you experienced humans successfully going back to the past to reclaim something of value that was left behind as a result of the relentless movement toward new ideas and new possibilities?

During the 2000 year history of Christianity leaders have often come together to create doctrines, creeds, statements of faith and other formulations for the guidance of the faithful. When have you felt gratitude for this kind of disciplined guidance?

What are the key practices and expressions of your faith today that sustain and inspire you wherever you are, whatever you are doing?

To what extent do you think you are an Emergent Christian in the way that Phyllis Tickle is defining that in this series?

When do you feel that worship really works for you? What are the elements that seem to be most helpful for you in bringing you to a place of worshipfulness.

OPTION 1: THE TREASURES OF ORTHODOXY

Beginning Conversation

What experience do members of your group have of the Eastern Orthodox tradition of Christianity?

The Teaching

Read Paragraph 1 from the Opening Essay, then play the first portion of Session 4 on the DVD (end around 4:00).

Five Key Points from Phyllis's Teaching:

- At these 500-year swing points in history there is a tendency to go back and reclaim the precious jewels of an earlier period (those things that were good and worthy and got left behind).
- Emergence is doing that, but not by going back to Roman Catholicism and Protestantism (both overly hierarchical) but to Orthodoxy.
- Historically, the Great Schism of 1054 created a rupture not only of Empire but between Eastern Greek language Orthodox Christianity and Latin language Western Roman Catholicism.
- For a thousand years the West has lived under a theology that is sharply different from the East.
- Emergence is drawing on the Orthodoxy that accrued before the Great Schism and beginning to re-introduce not just the theology but also the praxis.

Group Response to the Teaching

What do you think might be some of the treasures that Emergence Christianity could reclaim from Orthodoxy?

OPTION 2: FILIOQUE AND PERICHORESIS

Beginning Conversation

What has been your experience of the doctrine of the Trinity? For example, is it something you have struggled to understand? Is it a concept that you have appreciated for its capacity to explain simply something complex and mysterious?

The Teaching

Read paragraphs 4 and 5 from the Opening Essay, then play the second portion of Session 4 on the DVD (running from approximately 8:45 to around 14:20).

Group Response to the Teaching

There is a shift in understanding of the Trinity from a triangular, hierarchical model in which *filioque* is a key word and element to something more fluid that Phyllis identifies as *perichoresis*. This is a critical development in emergent thought. Take time as a group to be clear with one another about the shift from Trinity as filioque to Trinity as perichoresis that she is presenting.

To really incarnate the dramatic shift that is represented by filioque to perichoresis you could work with large sheets of paper and coloured crayons and pastels. Use the page and the colours to represent the transition from the rigidity of the Eastern and Western triangles to the fluidity of the dance of the red, blue and yellow flames. Try incorporating your own images and words onto your pages.

The members of the small group meeting with Phyllis each respond in their own ways to her teaching. Note the diversity of responses that they have made, then add your own responses to Phyllis's teaching and the group's reflections:

Kim:
- *There has always been a challenge to introduce children to the notion of the Trinity.*
- *I love that the concept of the Trinity is both so simple and yet so complex.*
- *It reminds me of the movement of molecules—the intersecting circles as well as the whole.*

Carolyn:
- *The dance of perichoresis keeps hierarchy from getting reestablished.*

China:
- *This is a further confirmation that we are being drawn away from two-dimensional toward multi-dimensional ways of describing sacred mystery. It presents a more human face.*
- *We want to pin down mystery with diagrams; perichoresis keeps us from doing that.*

James:
- *We talked in an earlier session about going into the Age of The Spirit. I wonder if that's the aspect of the Trinity that we haven't over-emphasized yet. You can look at Pentecostalism as the tip of the iceberg. The Spirit is everything… I would love to see us have a balance: this three-dimensionality— this sense that we are stuck in the middle of the Trinity—you can never quite get your bearings. I think that, ultimately, that's where you should be, that's the healthy place to be. It's a paradox: you're grounded when you're not grounded! You're always trying to reorient yourself (as you turn like a gyroscope).*
- *Emergence is going to over-emphasize the Spirit. We'll go through that phase where the Spirit is everything and the Father and the Son are under-emphasized.*

OPTION 3: NOTHING SAYS RESURRECTION LIKE CHOCOLATE! (INCARNATIONAL WORSHIP)

Beginning Conversation

When have you experienced incarnational worship, that is, worship that is "in your body," worship that connects with your senses, worship that connects with the fullness of who you are—body, mind and spirit?

The Teaching

Read paragraphs 2 and 3 from Phyllis's opening essay, then play the third section of Session 4 on the DVD (from approximately 14:20 to around 22:50).

The members of the small group with Phyllis add these reflections:

China:

- *I don't want a religion where I can't connect kinesthetically.*

Kim:

- *The musical instruments in worship play me. I literally 'feel' the music.*

James:

- *There's a reason we love incense. There's a reason why church music was the music for so long.*

James:

- *The church has always realized that if you can't feel it, it's not really happening.*

Kim:

- *People want to go on that journey down that centre aisle…to receive the bread…to light the candle…to walk up those steps… to get in touch with the wisdom of the ancients. There's something about the walk!*

Group Response to the Teaching

Phyllis mentions several mediums of incarnational worship: *dance, painting (easels), pottery wheels and clay, colours and costumes with an Eastern aesthetic, icons* and *liturgical dance.* This is just a beginning list of the kind of forms and disciplines that might be engaged in order to move worship out of our heads and hearts and into our flesh (in-carnation).

- What does your congregation do to facilitate incarnational worship?
- What possibilities emerge for you from this focused discussion?
- How could you go beyond just encouraging more worship experiences that engage the whole person?

Phyllis says that in Emerging theology there is a refusal to recognize the dichotomy of spirit and body—an assertion that this is a false dichotomy. What do you as a group think of this statement? Is it true that your spirituality has been more cerebral than embodied? When have you had experiences of spirit and body truly not be separate but fully integrated? What was that like? How could you have more of that?

OPTION 4: BELONGING, BEHAVING AND BELIEVING

Beginning Conversation

As you think about your participation in a faith community, what weight do these three words carry in your relationship with that community: *behave, believe* and *belong?*

The Teaching

Read paragraph 6 from Phyllis's opening essay, then play the fourth portion of Session 4 on the DVD (from approximately 22:50 to about 29:30).

Group Response to the Teaching

You have heard Phyllis speak and write in this way:

> *Up to now traditional Christianity has said, "Believe this, then behave in this way, and then we will let you belong." Every expression of Emergence Christianity says the opposite: "You belong first, regardless; then you behave in these ways; and perhaps in time you will believe." It's only possible to go with belong…behave…believe if you have the freedom to say, "I can't say what God is. I know God intimately, but I cannot articulate what God is nor would I presume to do so."*

In what ways has your own journey of faith been reflective of these three key words (*behave, believe* and *belong*)? When have you noticed the order of those words shifting as your faith has grown and changed?

The members of the small group interacting with Phyllis each respond to her teaching concerning the shift from *believe…behave… belong* to *belong…behave…believe*. In what ways is the dynamic of these three words reflected in the life of your congregation? Do you lean more toward traditional or emergent in the way that Phyllis has defined those terms? If you were to choose to be a community based on *belong…behave…believe*, what would you need to do for that to be fully incarnated in the life of the congregation?

OPTION 5: WHERE ARE WE NOW?

Beginning Reflection

You might have participated in four sessions now. Most of what has been offered will have been quite new to you unless you have spent time with Phyllis Tickle in other settings. So it's appropriate that at the end of Session 4, with two more sessions to go, we stop and take stock of where we are in this emerging process.

Without talking about it, stop and notice what you are feeling and thinking about all these ideas, about the process of experiential exploration, and about the kind of world and church that is being uncovered through Phyllis's teaching. Now go on to the teaching section…

The Teaching

Watch the fifth and final portion of the DVD for Session 4, beginning with approximately 29:30.

Notice the words and expressions used by the members of the small group with Phyllis:

- *I feel hopeful.*
- *I feel peaceful.*
- *I feel comforted.*
- *I'm in awe at the vastness of ideas being presented.*
- *I recognize a universal longing to which we are turning our attention.*
- *I feel like Jeremiah 31: "The plans I have for you to prosper and give you hope for the future."*
- *We're rediscovering something as Christians that is profoundly important and that can complete us in a certain way; something that has been missing and that I have longed for for a long time.*
- *I want very big arms and an open mind.*

Group Response to the Teaching

From all that you have experienced so far in this series of programs what stands out as the most challenging, the most hopeful, and the most inspiring.

What question would you want to ask Phyllis Tickle if she were right here in your group? What responses do other members of your group have to your question?

What do you think is going to be different for you as a result of your participation in this study group?

OPTION 6: CLOSING AS IF IT MATTERS

Go around the circle and have people complete these stems as they are able (it's always an option to pass):

I know that I belong when...

The kinds of practices (behaviors) that really deepen my faith are...

I know that *believing* really means *beloving* when...

SESSION | 5

HOW THEN SHALL WE LIVE?

ESSAY FIVE BY PHYLLIS TICKLE

1. As we will see shortly in viewing the video for Session 5, unsettling as is the question of "Where now is our authority? (or as Emergence Christians prefer to say, "How then shall we live?"), there are two or three other questions that besiege us almost as harshly as does the one of authority. The only difference is that the authority question always arises and always must be answered anew every time we pass through one of our semi-millennial "hinges of history." The concomitant and almost as insistent other questions, on the other hand, are unique to the hinge or tsunami in which they occur.

2. The Great Emergence has brought us three such questions. One of them requires an answer only from Emergence Christians. The other two, however, require two answers that must be resolved in such a way as to be harmonious, one with the other. That is, two of the three questions that the Great Emergence has raised require two answers: one appropriate for political use for all citizens of the Great Emergence and the other, appropriate simultaneously for Emergence Christians who are also citizens of the larger culture.

3. If all of this sounds difficult, it is. All three of our Emergence-born questions raise wrenching issues. The two that require complementary but dual answers are especially so. In all three cases, however, as we work our way through the hard business of discovering new ways of being and believing, we at least have the consolation, counsel and example of the Archbishop of Canterbury, Rowan Williams.

4. Since Emergence Christianity as an obvious and informing part of the general conversation came last to North America, it is one of the mischievous ironies of history that it should have been a North American who issued its clearest declaration of positioning and its most powerful battle cry; but that is exactly what happened. In the same way that Luther's 95 Theses on the door of the castle church in Wittenberg sounded the declaration of change that was the Great Reformation, so *A Generous Orthodoxy*, written by Brian McLaren and published in 2004, became the declaration of immutable change for the Great Emergence.

5. The story goes that shortly before *Orthodoxy* was to be released to the public, Dr. Williams received a galley (pre-publication copy) of McLaren's declaration and read it while he was on a plane. When he had

completed reading the galley, the Archbishop was so convicted and persuaded that, as he was to say later, all he wanted to do was buy up all the copies of *Orthodoxy* that were about to be released, hire a fleet of airplanes, and air-drop those copies all over the UK because, he said, "This is what our people must hear."

6. Air-lifting books across a whole country was, of course, not feasible nor, one must assume, was it ever actually a part of the Archbishop's intentions. Instead, he returned to Lambeth and opened the Office of Fresh Expressions, making the Anglican Communion the first of the established traditions to engage Emergence Christianity in an open and affirming way. Fresh Expressions was soon co-sponsored and co-administered by the Methodist Church in England, making Methodism the first established branch of Protestantism to move out in support and welcoming assistance. As a result, one of the distinct and most clearly definable bodies within the spectrum of Emergence Christianity is Fresh Expressions and the hundreds of groups, gathering, nodes and pods all over the English-speaking world that function in conjunction with its counsel and accommodations.

7. The important thing for us here, though, is not so much to rejoice in how two communions have already begun to work with Emergence Christians, but rather to hear as well something else that Archbishop Williams is often quoted as having said.

8. When he was questioned about his establishment, using Church funds and Church space, of the Fresh Expressions office—indeed, one might say when he was challenged about that use on his part of Church resources—he answered his critics with what may be the most profound and certainly prescient words possible. He spoke in terms of the Church of England, but any one of us can substitute with equal appropriateness the name of the institutional form of church to which we belong.

9. What Archbishop Williams is quoted as saying is: "My brothers and sisters in Christ, if we think we are here to save the Church of England, may God have mercy on our immortal souls. We are here to serve the Kingdom of God and, behold, God is doing a new thing among us."

10. We are *not* here to serve or save a church or an institution, but to serve the Kingdom of God in this strange and pivotal time of ours in which, behold, "God is doing a new thing among us."

11. These are words to ponder, but so also is the action that has accompanied them, an action or series of on-going actions in which the established church has found ways to welcome this new thing as sibling and co-inheritor of the family's life and future.

12. Given all of this, how can we pledge ourselves to any less? That is the fourth question.

BEFORE THE SESSION

Many participants like to come to the group conversation after considering individually some of the issues that will be raised. The following five reflective questions are intended to open your minds, memories and emotions regarding some aspects of this session's topic. Use the space provided here to note your reflections.

When do you feel like your Christian allegiance pulls you one way and your membership in society pulls you in another?

When were you last confronted by a situation that required you to think about what it means to be human?

What is the meaning for you of Jesus' crucifixion?

What physical things remind you of the reality of our "soul connection" with God?

What "new thing" do you perceive God doing in your midst?

OPTION 1: THE RETURN OF DUAL CITIZENSHIP

Beginning Conversation

Under what circumstances are you most aware of living "a divided life," pulled one way by your loyalty to your country and all that it stands for, and another way by your Christian conviction?

The Teaching

Read the first two paragraphs of Phyllis's opening essay for this session, then watch the first portion of Session 5 on the DVD (up to about 6:30).

Note the key points that Phyllis Tickle is making in understanding this issue of "dual citizenship":

- In addition to having to respond to the every-500-year question (*Where now is our authority?*), there are three other questions to answer this time around. (This session addresses these three questions.)
- Two of the questions require two answers, one from church or ecclesial point of view, the other from a secular or political point of view. Every Christian has to find an answer that is compatible with both points of view.

- Historically, until 50 years ago, this conflict between a religious and a secular point of view was not in the awareness of most Americans. As Phyllis says:
  — *If you were a good Englishman, you were a good Anglican. If you were a good German, you were a good Lutheran. If you were a good Netherlander, you were a good Reformer. If you were a good American, you were a good Christian. It was inconceivable that the state would not form itself around your pre-conceptions because in each case the majority of us belonged to that persuasion. We knew what we thought: God said it, and so we're gonna do it! So the state had to conform to some extent. Then you hit the beginning of the unravelling...*
- World War II accelerates the process of unravelling as we become more aware of the world.
- There is an aggressive reaction to this unravelling from evangelicalism: "To be American you had to be Christian. If it weren't Christian, you couldn't vote for it."
- And then by the early 90s there is a counter-reaction on the part of "thinking people" as there is a gradual awareness that we are indeed dual citizens and have to answer the key questions from both points of view.

Group Response to the Teaching

Phyllis sums up her analysis and makes it more personal for us when she says: "You never want to belong to a religion that's socially acceptable; it's bad for your soul. We no longer do; but our grandparents did." In what ways does her analysis ring true for you and your family?

Right back at the beginning of her analysis, in speaking of Constantine's political strategies, Phyllis said:

> Constantine (the Roman Emperor from 306 to 337 CE) was a shrewd politician. For the Constantinian political program to work he had to get in bed with the church, and the church got in bed with him. For the first 250 years of the church you find our forebears in the faith absolutely opposed to Rome in every way. That begins to erode. By the time you get to 312, you've got this engagement dance. By the time you get to 340 we're actually married in every way and we stay married until about 50 years ago.

Essentially Phyllis is saying that Emergence Christianity calls us back to a pre-Constantinian relationship with the secular society in which all Christians find themselves living both within and apart from the dominant society. How does that call sit with you?

OPTION 2: WANTED: A THEOLOGY OF RELIGION

Beginning Conversation

What would make it possible for you to practice your religion in a way that has integrity for you while people of other religions in your community practice theirs, without ever needing to resort to violence?

The Teaching

Watch the second portion of Session 5 on the DVD (from approximately 6:30 to about 14:30).

Phyllis is clear in declaring:

> We do not have a theology of religion and we cannot go much longer without arriving at one.

She is also helpful in spelling out specifically what that means for us today:

> We have to arrive at some sort of understanding that allows us, as devout and practicing Christians, to function in a polity that is composed of folk who are members of other often disparate and sometimes antagonistic faiths who are equally devout and equally persuaded, without coming into civil strife and without destroying the polity.

> We have to find a way for good Christians to create a polity that allows for everybody without violating our Christian particularity.

Group Response to the Teaching

Phyllis talks in some detail about Christianity and Islam. She notes that Islam, just like Christianity, is incredibly diverse in its identity and expression. We cannot treat it as a monolith. How much do you collectively know about Islam as a religion and Muslims as a faith community in your area?

China speaks passionately about the human dimension that we want to have inform the shaping of a new theology of religion:

> The only way to build tolerance is to take it to a one-on-one, flesh meeting flesh, touching, heartbeat level. The problem is that so much of this has been black and white, in our heads, an idea. But ideas aren't people. At the end of the day we're just all people; we're all just sharing the same space, the same air. We forget that and that's when we lose our humanity; we lose our religion; we lose the true soul of Christianity.

In the spirit of China's declaration, one way of developing a theology of religion would be through practice rather than through discussion; that is, by uncovering a theology of religion through your ongoing relationship with another faith community such as an Islamic one. Can you think of another faith community in your area whose members might be open to an invitation to explore with you how to be God's diverse people within the political, economic and social reality of your secular community?

Phyllis identifies two of many dilemmas in this matter of a theology of religion. One is the requirement in some Christian denominations that members be active in bringing others into their faith (proseletyzing), and the other is the presence of contradictory statements in the Bible concerning Jesus' claims to be the only way to God. How would you deal with these two issues when it comes to shaping a theology of religion that meets the criteria Phyllis states above in the Teaching part of Option 2?

Beginning Conversation

What does it mean to be human?

The Teaching

Watch the third portion of Session 5 on the DVD (from approximately 14:30 to about 23:50).

Note, once again, how Phyllis as a popular historian and journalist, quickly gives us an overview of a period of history relative to a particular issue that she is exploring. In this case her concern is summed up in these statements:

- We don't know what a human being is.
- We are in the business of saving souls and we are clueless about what one is.

...and in these questions:

- How can you decide end-of-life issues if you don't know whose life you are ending?
- How can you make decisions about penal codes, abortion and bioengineering if you don't know what a human being is?
- What are we?

In her overview, Phyllis names a number of prominent thinkers who were and are concerned about these questions: Rene Descartes (1596–1650), Franz Mesmer (1734–1815), William James (1842–1910), Sigmund Freud (1856–1939), Carl Jung (1875–1961), Alan Turing (1912–1954), Timothy Leary (1920–1996), Ken Wilber (b. 1949), Ray Kurzweil (b. 1948).

Note: The fact that they are all men doesn't mean that women were not also considering these significant questions; we just know that in the journey of human consciousness in our Euro-centered civilization that the consciousness of women hasn't been afforded the same respect and visibility as that of men. If the emergence of woman leadership in our faith communities is anything to go by, the 21st Century list of prominent thinkers and activists will reflect more justly the consciousness of women as well as men.

Group Response to the Teaching

What do you make of Phyllis's challenge that we don't know anymore what a human being is? What do you say sets humans apart from other forms of life?

When have you found yourself confronted by issues in areas such as euthanasia, abortion, reproductive technology and bioengineering, unable to make your mind up because our collective awareness of what it means to be human is so much less clear than it was at other times in history?

In response to Phyllis saying, "We are in the business of saving souls and we are clueless about what one is," Kim observes:

When we talk about the soul, I remember reading something from Parker Palmer who was talking about the soul like a soft animal barely born needing a safe place to come out. I think that we know something of God and we know something of our own souls even though we can't really describe that; it's just a knowing that's there. When I was a child looking in my grandparent's windowsill, there was a beautiful cobalt blue glass vase. I was so captivated by it! It could look opaque and then there'd be a little moonlight and I could see into it. It was beautiful! When I think of the soul that's what I think of. When I think of God that's what I think of.

What do you think of when you think of a soul?

What is at the centre of human identity?

What are you learning about your humanity from your relationships with people here in this group as well as in other places?

OPTION 4: OUT WITH THE ATONEMENT!

Beginning Conversation

The *doctrine of the atonement* teaches that God initiated the life, suffering and death of Jesus in order to save humanity and to bring humanity into a new relationship with God. There are many ways that this is expressed, this being one of the most common: *Jesus died to save us from our sins.* What place has the theory of atonement had in your journey of faith? Where do you stand in relation to it today?

The Teaching

Watch the fourth and final section of Session 5 on the DVD (beginning at approximately 23:50).

Once again Phyllis offers historical perspective on the origin of this doctrine that has played such a significant role in the lives of millions of Christians over the last 900 years. You will hear about the following 'Fathers of the Church' in her presentation:

- Origen of Alexandria (185–254 CE)
- Augustine of Hippo (354–430 CE)
- Anselm of Canterbury (1033–1109)
- Peter Abelard (1079–1142)

Group Response to the Teaching

Notice that the reason Phyllis is bringing the issue of the Atonement into this study is because Emergence Christians do not accept the notion that an omnipotent God couldn't find a better way to be reconciled with humanity than through the sacrifice of his own child. Given this measure, where do you stand in relation to Emergence Christianity? Would you also say, with Emergents, "That's not the kind of Daddy I need!"

Many Christians have never had the opportunity to stop and consider how easily we slip into the language and influence of atonement thinking. Take copies of your hymn book and prayer book and look through it for expressions of the kind of sin-and-salvation theology that is rooted in the Doctrine of the Atonement. For example, there is a traditional Holy Week hymn that appears in most mainline denominational hymnbooks with words by Cecil Frances Alexander: "There is a Green Hill Far Away." If possible, find and read the words of this hymn. Notice how atonement theology is woven throughout.

OPTION 5: THE FOURTH QUESTION

Beginning Conversation

Who would miss your church if it suddenly disappeared?

The Teaching

Read the rest of the Phyllis's opening essay, that is, from paragraph three to the end. Notice how, in the latter part of this essay, Phyllis has turned from overview and exposition to advocacy and challenge beginning with the prophetic actions of Archbishop Rowan Williams.

Her challenge to us:
- We are not here to serve or save a church or an institution, but here to serve the Kingdom of God in this strange and pivotal time of ours in which, behold, God is doing a new thing among us.
- Let us all participate in the on-going actions in which established Church is finding ways to welcome this new thing (Emergence) as sibling and co-inheritor of the family's life and future.

Given all of this, *how can we pledge ourselves to this future?* That is the fourth question.

Group Response to the Teaching

Phyllis quotes the Archbishop of Canterbury, Rowan Williams, as saying, "My brothers and sisters in Christ, if we think we are here to save the Anglican Church, may God have mercy on our immortal souls. We are here to serve the Kingdom of God and, behold, God is doing a new thing among us." What new thing do you perceive God doing in your midst that is about making God's realm a universal reality?

To what extent are you as a congregation in the business of "saving your church" rather than bringing in the realm of God? What's your way, as a community, of maintaining a church presence where you are while staying focused on the larger call to make visible God's compassion for all things, and God's passion for justice?

OPTION 6: CLOSING AS IF IT MATTERS

Prayer of Alcuin of York
(c. 735–804, an English scholar, ecclesiastic, poet and teacher)

Give us, O Lord, we pray,
firm faith,
unwavering hope,
a passion for justice.

Pour into our hearts
the Spirit of Wisdom and Understanding,
the Spirit of Counsel and Spiritual Strength,
the Spirit of Knowledge and True Compassion,
the Spirit of Wonder in all Your Works.

Light Eternal,
shine in our hearts;
Power Eternal,
deliver us from evil;
Wisdom Eternal,
scatter the darkness of our ignorance;
Might Eternal,
have mercy on us.

Grant that we may ever seek your face
with all our heart, soul and strength.
And in your infinite mercy
bring us at last to the fullness of your presence
where we shall behold your glory and live your promised joys.
In the name of Jesus,
our body and blood,
our life and our nourishment.

Amen.

SESSION | 6

HALLMARKS OF EMERGENCE

ESSAY SIX BY PHYLLIS TICKLE

1. As we engage in the last of our six conversations, we consider a dozen or so characteristics and concepts that have become general hallmarks of Emergence Christianity. We will look, in other words, at ideas and patterns that form the body or major themes of the conversation which is Emergence Christianity at this point in its evolution.

2. It certainly would be enough and entirely worthy for us just to inform ourselves of all these things out of curiosity and perhaps general interest, but there is also the potential here in this last discussion for opening up more than that; for it is only as we understand one another that we discover how best to engage and support one another.

3. Always in the past, when the latinized world has passed through one of these tectonic shifts…one of these "Greats" of ours…there has been bloodshed of huge and wrenching proportions. If we manage to negotiate our way through the decades just ahead without engaging in any more fractional and religious and cultural warfare than that which we have already known, then it will be the first time in our history that we and our forebears have done so. Yet there is hope that we may indeed do just that, because this is the first time in latinized history that we have been

able to know and to discuss broadly and generally with one another what it is that is happening to us both as a body of Christians and as citizens of a culture in shift. To know, in this case anyway, is for all of us to be over half-way to the goal of being wise. To know, for us as Christians in the time of shift, can also be more. To know—if we allow it—is also to be half-way to the goal of being full of grace.

4. The established church in almost all of its presentations has begun finding ways to welcome and encourage Emergence Christianity. Sometimes that effort presents as establishing alternative ("alt") communions and groups within the larger body and facilities of an established congregation. Sometimes it means joining with other congregations to enable free-standing Emergence nodes, pods or groups to freely enjoy the transcendence of special worship services like festal Eucharists and choral prayers in the glory of traditional sacred space. Sometimes it is simply serving as center and conduit for a diaspora of such groups. Sometimes it means empowering and then enabling bi-vocationals, tent-makers, circuit riders and deacons to minister to the numerically small and scattered Emergence groups and house

churches. Sometimes it means freeing paid clerical staff to plant new groups and/or sometimes simply "be" in places where loose and fluid gatherings occur around pub theology, whether in a pub, a Starbucks or a neighborhood diner. Sometimes it means offering support—physical, financial, spiritual—to neo-monastic groups as they struggle, like Julian of Norwich, to live in constant obedience while building themselves into the protecting outer wall of established church.

5. The list goes on and on. But in all of its possibilities, both listed and not included here, three things need saying. The first is to reiterate that every time we have passed through one of our upheavals, whatever presentation of the faith that had held hegemony has had to drop back and reconfigure. It did *not* die or cease to be of importance (and, by the way, it won't). It simply had to change and go on in new ways so that the faith itself could grow and spread geographically and demographically. That is what is happening now. Anglicanism is not dead. Protestantism is not dead. Roman Catholicism is not dead. Orthodoxy is not dead. They've just gained a new fellow-traveler in the living and spreading of the faith.

6. Second, despite how attractive many of us may find our adaptations and offers of support to be, there are many, many Emergence churches, groups, bodies etc. that will want no part of them or us. They are worthy, however, of our prayers wherever we discover them to be.

7. Third, it is true that in almost all cases, the flow of cash is a one-way phenomenon. The money to support and nurture will not be coming back with or without interest in most cases. Rowan Williams is right about that: This is not about church, but rather it is about Kingdom. If we remember that, then as Julian herself said, "It will be well, and all things shall be well."

BEFORE THE SESSION

Many participants like to come to the group conversation after considering individually some of the issues that will be raised. The following five reflective questions are intended to open your minds, memories and emotions regarding some aspects of this session's topic. Use the space provided here to note your reflections.

What qualities of Emergence Christianity have most appealed to you so far in Phyllis's presentations?

What motivates you to act in the ways you do as you go about the ordinary things of life from day to day?

What lifestyle choices do you wish you could change in some way?

What are the ways that you know that you are taking your life seriously and not coasting on conventionality to the end of your life?

Emergence, even in its name, is clearly all about change and transformation. How well do you handle change? What have been some of the great "change accomplishments" of your life? What makes it easier for you to be engaged in change?

OPTION 1: A QUICK REVIEW

Beginning Conversation

As you come into this session having participated in some of the previous five sessions, what is the dominant sense you have of Emergence Christianity?

The Teaching

Watch the first portion of Session 6 on the DVD (up to about 6:35).

Read paragraphs 1, 2 and 3 of the Phyllis's opening essay for this session.

Phyllis quickly reviews eight significant hallmarks of Emergence Christianity that have been dealt with in previous sessions, prior to going on to five others that she has not addressed up to this point. First, let's summarize the eight:

- Emergence Christianity is deeply *incarnational* in its practice. The body will be engaged as well as the heart and mind.
- Emergence Christianity is *actualist* rather than literalist in its approach to Scripture; there is actual truth beyond the facts.
- Emergence Christianity calls for radical *obedience*: the call to "give it all up for me" is to be taken seriously.
- Emergence Christianity includes a new understanding of the Trinity *(Perichoretic)*.
- Emergence Christianity is *deinstitutionalized*, therefore no Bishops, a redefinition of other traditional forms of leadership.

- Emergence Christianity is *nonhierarchical*.
- Emergence Christianity is *resistant to owning real estate*.
- Emergence Christianity is *transitory* in its very nature, taking seriously the unencumbered itinerancy of Jesus.

Group Response to the Teaching

As you look at this quick review of Emergence characteristics, which of them appeal to you?

OPTION 2: GOD SENSE OR COMMON SENSE?

Beginning Conversation

When you are engaged in "action for justice," "acts of environmental recovery," or anything else that just makes good common sense given the overwhelming needs of the world, what motivates you?

The Teaching

Watch the second portion of Session 6 on the DVD (from approximately 6:35 to about 12:05).

Phyllis is making it very clear that Emergent Christians distinguish between an act of compassion or kindness that is done apart from Christian commitment and one that is done by a person who is a follower of Christ.

Group Response to the Teaching

What is the distinction that Phyllis is making?

How does that distinction play out in your own action in your community and in the world?

In what ways might the Emergent attitude to Christian action in society and the world have an influence on you as you respond to the needs you encounter every day?

OPTION 3: TAKING OUR LIVES SERIOUSLY

Beginning Conversation

Jesus calls us to be engaged in his mission of transformation from the time we get up in the morning until we go to bed at night. How are you doing at that? In what ways does it feel like *Mission Impossible?*

The Teaching

Play the third portion of Session 6 on the DVD (beginning at approximately 12:05 to about 26:35), then read paragraph 4 of Phyllis's opening essay.

In this section Phyllis presents two other hallmarks of Emergent Christianity:

- *Neo-monasticism*: the vowed community (expressed as house church or common table/common purse or celibacy or simply a rule of life)
- *Life as Mission:* mission is everything I do from the moment I get up until I brush my teeth and go to bed—never a program

On the DVD, the facilitator then proposes that the question before the group members, given all the hallmarks of Emergent Christianity presented by Phyllis, is "How then shall we live?" Carolyn, James, China and Kim respond to this question from a number of perspectives:

- lifestyle choices
- living without fear
- life as mission
- reclaiming Christianity as our way
- the place of love
- the power and practice of change

Group Response to the Teaching

As you listen to Phyllis's presentation and to the personal responses of the group members, what question emerges for you in relation to your own life? How might you go about addressing that question in a way that "takes your life seriously"?

Note the range of creative options for the established church that are named by Phyllis in paragraph 4 of the Opening Essay:

- The established Church in almost all of its presentations has begun finding ways to welcome and encourage Emergence Christianity.
- Sometimes that effort presents as establishing alternative communions and groups within the larger body and facilities of an established congregation.
- Sometimes it means joining with other congregations to enable free-standing Emergence nodes or pods or groups to freely enjoy the transcendence of special worship services like festal eucharists and choral prayers in the glory of traditional sacred space.
- Sometimes it is simply serving as center and conduit for a diaspora of such groups.
- Sometimes it means empowering and then enabling bi-vocationals, tent-makers, circuit riders and deacons to minister to the numerically small and scattered Emergence groups and house churches.
- Sometimes it means freeing paid clerical staff to plant new groups and/ or sometimes simply "be" in places where loose and fluid gatherings occur around pub theology, whether in a pub, a Starbucks or a neighborhood diner.
- Sometimes it means offering support— physical, financial, spiritual—to neo-monastic groups as they struggle, like Julian of Norwich, to live in constant obedience while building themselves into the protecting outer wall of established church.

Which of these have already, in some form, been part of the life of your congregation or parish? Which ones might you consider taking on in some way now that they are on the table? If your group wanted to initiate something with an Emergence flavor, how would you go about that? What will you do together?

OPTION 4: FINAL WORDS

Beginning Conversation

What are you experiencing in thought and feeling as you come to the end of these six sessions?

The Teaching

Play the fourth and final portion of Session 6 on the DVD (beginning at approximately 26:35), then read paragraphs 5, 6 and 7 of Phyllis's opening essay.

Note the summary statements of the four participants as they come to the end of these six conversations:

James:

> I've gone from anxiety to peace to stability to excitement. I'm not scared anymore!

Kim:

> It's been enlightening for me to see this as part of something happening in our religion and culture. It gives me lots of hope to see us engage and become more serious about who we are as God's people.

Carolyn:

> It's sparked in me a desire to speak more specifically about what's going on in our congregation, not just in Christianity as a whole.

China:

> I feel like someone's handed me a map. There's an "X marks the spot." I don't feel as lost, as out to sea in this grand question. I feel hopeful not only for the future of the church, for the future of Jesus Christ in the world, but also for me and where I'm headed."

Group Response to the Teaching

What intentions do you carry away from your participation in this series?

What support will enable you to pursue those intentions with hope?

For what do you feel grateful as you come to the end of this journey in community?

OPTION 5: CLOSING AS IF IT MATTERS

As we come to the end of this series of six conversations we will turn to the prophet Isaiah who offers us a sense of a timeless Spirit and eternal wisdom from his living 2,800 years ago:

Isaiah 42:9

See, the former things have come to pass,
  and new things I now declare;
before they spring forth,
  I tell you of them.

Isaiah 43:19

I am about to do a new thing;
  now it springs forth, do you not perceive it?
I will make a way in the wilderness
  and rivers in the desert.

Isaiah 48:6

You have heard; now see all this;
  and will you not declare it?
From this time forward I make you hear new things,
  hidden things that you have not known.

Closing Prayer:

Brothers and sisters, let us go from
      this circle of sharing and
insight,
Alert to all that springs forth that we
did not shape ourselves,
Attentive to ways and waters in the
wilderness where we thought there
was no life,
And ready to declare, in a spirit of
love, all the new things that have
been made known to us.
Let us go, knowing that we are never
alone.
God is always with us.
Thanks be to God.
Amen.

Phyllis Tickle

Tim Scorer